NEIGHBORHOOD CHOICES

DATE DUE

Neighborhood Choices

SECTION 8 HOUSING VOUCHERS AND RESIDENTIAL MOBILITY

David P. Varady
Carole C. Walker

Edward J.
Bloustein School
of Planning and Public Policy

Center for Urban Policy Research—CUPR Press
Edward J. Bloustein School of Planning and Public Policy
Rutgers, The State University of New Jersey
New Brunswick, New Jersey

HD
7293
·V37
2007

Published by the CENTER FOR URBAN POLICY RESEARCH
Edward J. Bloustein School of Planning and Public Policy
Rutgers, The State University of New Jersey
Civic Square • 33 Livingston Avenue
New Brunswick, New Jersey 08901-1982

Printed in the United States of America

Library of Congress Cataloging-in-Publication Data

Varady, David P.
   Neighborhood choices : Section 8 housing vouchers and residential mobility / David P.
Varady, Carole C. Walker.
      p. cm.
   Includes bibliographical references and index.
   ISBN 0-88285-180-2 (alk. paper)
   ISBN 978-0-88285-180-8 (alk. paper)
      1. Housing subsidies—United States. 2. Housing policy—United States. 3. Residential
mobility—United States. 4. Housing—Resident satisfaction—United States. 5. Neighborhood
planning—United States. I. Walker, Carole C. II. Rutgers University. Center for Urban
Policy Research. III. Title.

   HD7293.V37 2007
   363.5'82'0973—dc22   2005046923

Cover design: Helene Berinsky

To our families

About the Authors

David P. Varady is professor of planning in the College of Design, Art, Architecture, and Planning at the University of Cincinnati. He has published numerous books and articles on residential mobility, public housing, and housing vouchers. His most recent edited book is *Desegregating the City: Ghettos, Enclaves, and Inequality* (State University of New York Press, 2005).

Carole C. Walker, former assistant director of the Center for Urban Policy Research, has studied a broad range of public policy issues including housing, residential mobility, supportive services for low-income households, and land-use regulations. She is the author or co-author of numerous research reports, scholarly articles, three model land-use ordinances for the state of New Jersey, and a book, *The Subdivision and Site Plan Handbook.*

Contents

Tables

Chapter 2

Chapter 3

Figures

Preface

In 1970, the U.S. Department of Housing and Urban Development's (HUD's) Experimental Housing Allowance Program (EHAP), the precursor to today's Section 8 Housing Choice Voucher Program, set out to design a program whereby housing assistance would be tied to families instead of units. For the first time, families receiving federal assistance would choose where they would live in the private rental market, a complete departure from traditional public housing and other project-based housing assistance. As HUD (2000, 9) stated on the thirtieth anniversary of the program, "The hallmark of the Section 8 program is *residential choice and mobility*" (emphasis in the original).

From the program's inception, policymakers, Section 8 program administrators, and researchers were interested in the types of housing and neighborhoods the families chose and the factors that influenced those choices. They also wanted to know whether the receipt of Section 8 housing assistance and the location of the housing unit chosen by the families enabled them to improve their pre–Section 8 housing conditions, increase participation in the labor market, and improve their children's education.

Although the Section 8 program always encouraged mobility, in the late 1980s the program underwent a significant change with the implementation of "portability." Portability allows families to use the Section 8 assistance outside the jurisdiction of the housing authority where they receive the assistance. This concept of portability was eventually expanded to allow a family to move anywhere in the United States.

Initially, public housing authorities (PHAs) across the nation reacted negatively to the policy change, anticipating administrative nightmares as well as negative community and political repercussions if families could take their Section 8 assistance and move anywhere. Those fears were substantially lessened when few families took advantage of the portability option.

In the San Francisco Bay Area and, particularly, in Alameda County, California, it was a different story. There was enough portability in the San Francisco Bay Area that the Northern California/Nevada Executive Directors' Association decided to fund a study to examine its impact. The study, completed by Joseph Villarreal in early 1993, found that portability tended to occur between adjacent PHA jurisdictions and that the highest portability usage was occurring in Alameda County.

Alameda County, comprising thirteen cities, is the seventh largest county in California, with a population of approximately 1.44 million in 2000. The city of Oakland is the largest city in the county, and its population of 399,484 is made up of 69 percent minority citizens. In addition, Oakland has the highest poverty rate (19.4 percent) of the thirteen cities. There are five Alameda County PHAs (Alameda City, Alameda County, Berkeley, Livermore, and Oakland) operating Section 8 programs. Oakland administers the largest program, followed by Alameda County, which serves nine primarily suburban cities and the unincorporated portion of the county.

Beginning in late 1987 and continuing through June 1994, the Housing Authority of Alameda County (HACA) received more than 1,200 Section 8 families who used the portability feature to move from the jurisdictions of other PHAs. More than 77 percent of these families came from the Alameda County cities of Alameda, Berkeley, and Oakland; 60 percent were from Oakland alone. In a very short time, portable families had become 20 percent of Alameda County's Section 8 program. Rapid administrative changes were required to handle a workflow that could not have been predicted. This included staff training on the service needs of a different clientele (more urban and more black) and intensive communication with other PHAs to address different operating procedures, eligibility policies, and billing and payment requirements.

Despite the increased workload resulting from the influx of porting families, HACA started collecting data and studying the movement of Section 8 families from Oakland into HACA's jurisdiction. Joseph Villarreal, who had become an analyst at HACA in mid-1993, began to map Oakland's portability moves and to analyze the demographic characteristics of these families. He found that in 1994, 55 percent of the incoming Section 8 Oakland families moved to just 17 census tracts in Alameda County's jurisdiction. More startlingly, half the Section 8 Oakland portable families came from just eighteen census tracts in Oakland. The census tracts from which they had moved had poverty rates of slightly more than 20 percent, while those to which they had moved had poverty rates of less than 13 percent. More than 90 percent of the Oakland movers were black, and on average, they moved from census tracts that were 61 percent black to ones where blacks made up 11 percent of the total. There was no question that, on the basis of standard indicators, Oakland's portable families were experiencing positive mobility impacts.

At about the same time, the research results from the Gautreaux program in Chicago were being published and discussed in major newspapers and even on the television program *60 Minutes*. HUD launched mobility programs such as Moving to Opportunity (MTO) and Regional Opportunity Counseling, and the Urban Institute began doing research on housing mobility as a deconcentration strategy.

The Alameda County experience stood in sharp contrast to the MTO-type programs, for which families were carefully selected, counseled about the advantages of moving to the suburbs, driven to suburban neighborhoods, and given special security deposits and other supportive programs. Somehow, in Alameda County, the goals of these special mobility programs were being met through the normal utilization of the Section 8 program's portability mechanism and at *no* additional administrative cost. This was quite different from the costs being reported for the special mobility programs, which in some cases reportedly exceeded several thousand dollars per family.

But, nobody believed it! In early 1994, I had an occasion to meet with Alex Polikoff, considered by many to be the father of Gautreaux, and described Alameda County's experience. He was initially quite skeptical. He encouraged Kale Williams, who was organizing the first national conference on housing mobility, to visit Alameda County to find out what was really happening. That visit led to an invitation to speak at the conference and the inclusion of the "intriguing" Alameda County experience in the conference report (see Turner and Williams 1998).

Joseph Villarreal and I became convinced that the Alameda County experience deserved more rigorous research to determine if there were lessons that could be learned for the development of national mobility policies. When we submitted a grant proposal to officials in HUD's Policy Development and Research division, we were told that although they were interested in the subject, they thought that it would be best if an academic researcher with the appropriate background and experience were found to conduct the study.

At a 1996 HUD-sponsored public housing summit (HUD 1996), I spoke with David Varady about our Alameda County experience. David expressed interest in the topic, explaining that his current research on the vouchering out of distressed housing developments, which he was conducting with Carole Walker at the Center for Urban Policy Research at Rutgers University, might dovetail with an Alameda study. That is how the Alameda County experience came to be ably researched and documented by David Varady and Carole Walker.

At the time Varady and Walker conducted their study, portability had decreased dramatically as a result of the severe tightening of the rental market, due to the dot-com boom in the San Francisco Bay Area. In the past two years, however, the softening of the rental market has brought extensive portability back. There are currently 958 portable families in the Alameda County Section 8 program, and 714 of them are from Oakland. The housing authority adds, on average, 36 new Oakland portable families per month. Paralleling the prior experience, this occurs with no special counseling. The most significant change is that Joseph Villarreal is now the Section 8 director for the Oakland Housing Authority, making communication even easier!

With the growth of portability throughout the nation and especially in large urban areas, this book's analysis of mobility patterns is an important contribution to the mobility literature. Varady and Walker correctly question the common wisdom that special MTO-type programs are needed everywhere to achieve moves to low-poverty and low-minority areas. In addition, adding to the body of knowledge about the decision-making process families go through in making housing moves is also important for future program and policy development.

At a time when HUD's budget is being reduced and the Section 8 program is being targeted for significant funding reductions, it is critical that program funds be spent wisely and effectively. This book's research will inform mobility policies and program design to ensure that the Section 8 Housing Choice Voucher program achieves its program "hallmark" of residential choice and mobility for all program participants.

Ophelia B. Basgal
Executive Director
Housing Authority of the County of Alameda, California
February 2004

Acknowledgments

This book is the culmination of several years of rewarding work that began when we codirected two research studies supported by the U.S. Department of Housing and Urban Development (HUD) through contracts with the Center for Urban Policy Research (CUPR) at Rutgers University. HUD sought to determine whether families receiving HUD housing vouchers had been able to improve their housing and neighborhood conditions. Contract DU100C000005967, task order 004, investigated this issue related to the vouchering out of distressed developments; and contract DU100C000005967, task order 007, examined the outcomes for families receiving housing vouchers in Alameda County.

We would like, first, to express our thanks to Norman J. Glickman, former director at CUPR, for providing us with a collegial, supportive, and stimulating environment while we carried out our two research projects—David as a distinguished senior scholar on leave from the University of Cincinnati during the first study and part of the second, and Carole as a senior researcher and assistant director at CUPR. We would also like to thank HUD for its generous support. Our government technical monitors—John B. Carson, on the vouchering-out study, and Garland E. Allen, on the Alameda County study—and staff from HUD's Office of Policy Development and Research provided guidance and encouragement throughout our research on these projects.

The studies resulted in two reports to HUD and several journal articles. (The two reports are Varady and Walker 1998 and 2000a. Articles include Varady and Walker 1999a, 1999b, 2000b, 2003a, 2003b, and 2003c.) Revised versions of some of these articles have been used for this book. We appreciate the comments of several anonymous journal reviewers whose suggestions improved the articles. The analyses and opinions expressed in the reports and articles and in this book are ours and do not necessarily reflect the views and policies of HUD or the U.S. government.

Obviously, research of the magnitude of the two HUD studies benefited from the contributions of many people. We wish to thank our collaborators on the vouchered-out study: Kirk McClure, from the University of Kansas, who conducted the Kansas City case study; and Janet Smith-Heimer, of Bay Area Economics, who conducted the San Francisco case study. Their contributions were many and deserve special recognition. We were also fortunate to have the assistance of Edward Freeland, of Response Analysis Corporation, who skillfully directed the household survey of the vouchered-out residents. Xinhao Wang, a colleague of David's at the University of Cincinnati, and Elvin Wyly, a colleague of Carole's at CUPR, were especially helpful in performing the geographic information system analysis. Finally, we thank the CUPR support staff, especially Linda S. Hayes, who edited the HUD vouchering-out report, and the highly capable team of Rutgers graduate students who worked on this project, particularly Sherry Larkins and Sudha Maheshwari, for their contributions to the research.

For the Alameda County study, our sincere thanks to Ophelia Basgal, the director of the Housing Authority of Alameda County (HACA), and to her staff at HACA. Ophelia's belief that the Alameda experience warranted attention provided the original impetus for that study. She and Joseph Villarreal—the senior administrative analyst at HACA at the time of the study and currently the director of Section 8 at the Oakland Housing Authority—conducted important preliminary research on Section 8 portability in Alameda County; made valuable suggestions during the development of the survey instrument; participated in interviews on portability in Alameda County; helped the authors arrange interviews with other officials; and provided helpful comments on drafts of the final report.

Many others also deserve recognition for their contributions to the Alameda County study. Several researchers at Rutgers University played vital roles, particularly William Dolphin, computer specialist at CUPR; Michael Lahr, research professor at CUPR; and Lyna Wiggins, associate professor at the Edward J. Bloustein School of Planning and Public Policy. Michael Siegel at Rutgers Cartography prepared the maps. The household survey was ably conducted by Al Ronca, Marlon Forde, and Matthew Moffre at SRBI, Inc. Several graduate students at the Edward J. Bloustein School of Planning and Public Policy deserve thanks for their participation in the study: Jumin Song, Sudha Maheshwari, G. Sue Dziamara, and Nicole Hostettler. CUPR's Catherine R. Liapes and Anne Henoch edited the manuscript; and Shannon Darroch, also at CUPR, provided secretarial support.

The art of transforming our HUD research and journal articles into a final manuscript has progressed under the expert hands of Arlene Pashman, senior editor at the Center for Urban Policy Research Press in the Edward J. Bloustein School of Planning and Public Policy at Rutgers University. She has tirelessly overseen the production of the manuscript, and to her we owe a considerable debt. Thanks are also due to Robert W. Lake, editor of the CUPR Press, for his support of this book. We greatly appreciate his help and encouragement.

Finally, we would like to thank the hundreds of families in the vouchering-out and Alameda County case studies that took part in the household surveys. Their cooperation and willingness to be interviewed made both studies possible. We would also like to thank those we interviewed at the study sites, including key staff from the agencies involved, housing and planning officials, landlords, and relocation counselors, as well as other informants. In writing this book, we have sought to add to the literature on the experiences of families receiving housing assistance under the regular HUD programs. We hope it will suggest ways for policymakers to improve the implementation of housing programs for the benefit of families across the country.

David P. Varady
Carole C. Walker

Introduction

In the 1980s and 1990s, the federal government fundamentally changed its policy for housing poor people. Finding that significant numbers of families receiving housing assistance were concentrated in high-poverty inner-city neighborhoods, the U.S. Department of Housing and Urban Development (HUD) launched several initiatives to provide greater opportunities for families. Under the new approach, HUD moved away from project-based assistance, which tied housing assistance to specific units, to tenant-based housing subsidies, which families could use in housing of their own choice. The Section 8 housing certificate program was expanded to include vouchers that gave families wider geographic latitude in their search for housing. Mobility counseling was offered to families under the Regional Opportunity Counseling initiative, as well as in other programs, and the HOPE VI program began to revitalize and replace public housing with mixed-income housing.

Studies of housing mobility programs have shown the benefits for families that moved into more diverse and decent-quality residential areas. Research on the Gautreaux housing mobility program, for example, which was implemented in response to litigation brought by public housing residents in Chicago, has shown that movement to the suburbs has been accompanied by benefits for the participants. The Moving to Opportunity for Fair Housing Demonstration Program (MTO), which is under way in five metropolitan areas across the country, is testing these findings and exploring them in more depth; early results suggest improvements for families moving to more affluent areas.

The promising results of studies of Gautreaux and MTO have led some analysts to conclude that the United States needs a large-scale MTO strategy (e.g., see Orfield 1997). Both Gautreaux and MTO, however, combine mobility counseling with strict requirements that participants move to low-poverty—or, in the case of Gautreaux, low-minority—areas. Adopting such restrictive policies nationwide would be not only expensive but also difficult to implement. Other alternatives must be sought if more householders are to enjoy the benefits of deconcentrated housing.

This book addresses the central question of whether it is possible to achieve the benefits of housing mobility offered by the Section 8 program while maximizing the degree of choice for householders. Although Gautreaux and MTO have been examined in several studies, few recent studies—with the exception of Goetz's 2003 case study of the *Hollman v. Cisneros* litigation settlement in Minneapolis—have investigated the housing choices of residents in the regular Section 8 program. The need for information about the choices made by participants in the regular Section 8 program motivated the research presented here.

We wanted to find out what happens to families receiving vouchers that move without the benefit of intensive counseling or requirements to locate in low-poverty or low-minority areas. Where do they go? Will they choose to move to areas offering greater opportunities? What are the experiences of residents making the journey to more diverse neighborhoods? How do they fare? How can moves to better-quality neighborhoods be encouraged within the regular Section 8 program?

In this book, we focus on the experiences of families receiving Section 8 housing vouchers in two programs: (1) the "vouchering out" of four federally subsidized private developments, where the residents were given only a bit more counseling than is provided in the regular program; and (2) the Section 8 program in Alameda County, where many inner-city families in Oakland and Berkeley were moving to suburban locations in the county—unlike in other metropolitan areas, where households with vouchers rarely cross the city/suburban boundary.

Our work is based on research supported by HUD through contracts with the Center for Urban Policy Research at Rutgers University. Research on the vouchering-out study was carried out from 1995 to 1997; research on the Alameda study was carried out from 1997 to 2000. In both studies, we employed a multimethod research strategy, combining a review of published materials and other documents, key informant interviews, surveys of the residents, observations of the programs in action, geographic information system techniques, and statistical analyses.

We found in the vouchering-out study that the families were able to improve their housing and neighborhood conditions with only a bit more counseling and assistance than is provided in the regular Section 8 program. In the second study, we found that hundreds of families in the East Bay Area under the auspices of the Berkeley, Oakland, and Alameda County housing authorities had indeed used their Section 8 vouchers to move into suburban locations. We found that these families improved their housing and neighborhood conditions by suburbanizing, that they had done so without any special counseling programs, and that close working relationships among the three housing authorities had facilitated such moves. And we found that a shift to a large-scale MTO strategy would be not only expensive but also counterproductive. Many poor people do not want to live in the suburbs, and many of the poorest families lack the motivation and skills required to negotiate the suburban private market.

Given these positive findings, instead of a wide-scale implementation of MTO, a more incremental approach is needed, one that builds upon the regular Section 8 program. An improved Section 8 program could be combined with socioeconomic programs aimed at the root causes of poverty. Up to now, too little attention has been given to ways to improve the operation of the regular Section 8 housing voucher program. This book is aimed at reducing this gap in the literature.

Chapter 1 begins with a discussion of housing vouchers and the reasons for interest in the approach as a means of deconcentrating assisted housing. We review the significance of results from the Gautreaux and MTO programs and from research on the regular operation of the Section 8 voucher program. Finally, we summarize the research on the benefits of mixed-income neighborhoods for low-income families.

Chapter 2 introduces the vouchering-out study (the study methodology, the socioeconomic and housing market characteristics of the four cities, and differences in the vouchering-out process and in the relocation counseling). It then describes the housing search process of the vouchered-out residents (the duration and scope of the housing search, the level and nature of discrimination that residents experienced). Next, it examines the migration patterns of the residents and the impacts these patterns had on their quality of life. Despite the fact that many did not want to move at all, after the move, most felt that they had improved their housing and neighborhood conditions as a result of the move. Certain types of counseling did help families carry out their moves. Contrary to what was expected, however, those who moved farther and who lived in more sub-urban-like settings were not necessarily more likely to be satisfied with their housing.

Our discussion of the Alameda housing voucher study in chapter 3 begins with an overview of the East Bay area (including a description of the three housing authorities in the county) and a description of the methodology of the study—a comparative analysis of families making differ-ent locational choices after receiving their Section 8 vouchers. Probing into the families' experiences, our analysis of the housing search produces a sur-prising result: Families moving to the suburbs were no more likely to ex-perience problems in carrying out their housing search than were those making local moves. Similarly, in contrast to findings in previous research, those moving to the suburbs were no more likely to experience problems of adjustment at their new locations than were local movers. Even though they did not receive any special help from any of the housing authorities, these families actually fared quite well, and, in fact, were more likely to move into neighborhoods with higher incomes and property values than were local movers. Furthermore, those moving to the suburbs were more likely to perceive that they had experienced improvements in housing and neighborhood conditions; they especially felt a greater sense of safety.

Chapter 4 summarizes the lessons learned from the studies and of-fers suggestions for making the regular housing voucher program more effective in promoting wider housing choices by low-income families.

1

The Case for Housing Mobility

When the U.S. Department of Housing and Urban Development (HUD) introduced housing vouchers in the early 1980s, they were part of a broader HUD strategy to deconcentrate poverty and reduce the isolation of low-income families. Also included were efforts to disperse federally subsidized private housing and public housing on scattered sites in the suburbs. HUD's HOPE VI program, implemented in the 1990s, was aimed at revitalizing distressed public housing projects by redeveloping them as mixed-income communities and providing some of the residents with housing vouchers to be used in the private housing market. All these programs sought to provide wider housing opportunities for families and to improve the lives of the poor across multiple dimensions.

At the heart of HUD's broad strategy to deconcentrate housing assistance was an evolving conviction that providing housing to low-income families at inner-city locations had contributed to serious problems in many areas. William Julius Wilson (1987) argued that concentrated poverty leads to negative behavioral and attitudinal outcomes, an increased likelihood of unemployment, and lower levels of educational attainment. Living in a low-poverty neighborhood, advocates of deconcentration argued, can offer such advantages for low-income families as (1) access to good schools and other services; (2) the presence of adults who can serve as role models for acceptable behavior; (3) the absence of negative influences for peers, especially for teenagers; (4) informal networks to gain access to jobs and

Portions of this chapter are adapted from David P. Varady and Carole C. Walker, "Housing Vouchers and Residential Mobility," *Journal of Planning Literature* 18, 1: 17–30. © 2003 SAGE Publications. Reprinted by permission of SAGE Publications.

services; (5) low levels of crime and violence; and (6) physical access to jobs (Ellen and Turner 1997). Some poverty deconcentration advocates, such as Myron Orfield (1997), are so convinced by the neighborhood-effects hypotheses that they urge abandoning community development programs (those aimed at helping to improve housing and related social conditions in the inner city) because they anchor the poor to the inner city.

Now, just a little more than twenty years after the introduction of housing vouchers, we ask in this chapter whether housing vouchers and other housing mobility programs have achieved the presumed positive benefits for the poor.[1] Have these programs helped families move to better housing and neighborhoods and thereby make progress toward self-sufficiency?[2] We synthesize the results that have appeared in a wide variety of reports prepared for HUD and other agencies on the impact of the regular Section 8 program. We also examine the validity of some of the sociological assumptions underlying housing mobility programs, for example, that living in mixed-income communities can increase exposure to middle-class role models as well as to middle-class job networks. Too often, planners have treated these assumptions as established facts rather than as hypotheses to be tested.

We will see that housing mobility programs are not a panacea for urban poverty. Up to now, existing discussions of the benefits of housing mobility programs have relied on the Gautreaux and Moving to Opportunity for Fair Housing Demonstration (MTO) programs, two fairly small programs that have produced some positive results. But these programs are costly and have special requirements that cannot be easily expanded into national programs. Research on the operation of the regular Section 8 program both nationally and at the local level highlights problems facing voucher holders, but it also shows that well-managed programs can lead to meaningful improvements in housing and neighborhood conditions. In addition, research on social mixing provides limited support for the role model and social network hypotheses.

Our review of the literature therefore suggests that a housing mobility strategy based on an improved Section 8 voucher program offers advantages over the implementation of a national MTO-type effort. It would be more politically feasible; it would be less expensive; and it would provide the poor with choices (they would not be required to move to areas meeting specific socioeconomic criteria, as mandated in the MTO and Gautreaux programs). And though it might not address some of the root causes of urban poverty, such as the breakdown of the family unit, it would promote improvement in housing and neighborhood conditions, a more modest but nonetheless important goal.

Before reviewing the research evidence in support of these conclusions, we first describe in further detail the evolution of HUD's housing voucher program and the context in which wider objectives for the program emerged.

The Evolution of Housing Vouchers

Following the enactment of the Wagner-Steagall Housing Act in 1937 (U.S. Senate 1937), which created the framework for the public housing system, for more than thirty years housing policy in the United States emphasized project-based housing assistance. This type of assistance was tied to specific units, either in public housing projects or, later, in the form of subsidies that gave developers incentives to build housing for low-income people. Many of the projects and developments that were constructed before and after World War II were geographically concentrated in urban or transitional areas marked by high poverty rates, marginal housing, and mixed uses.

By the late 1960s, however, the problems attending the concentration of low-income families were of increasing concern across the country. HUD regulations restricted public housing to people with low incomes; those whose income rose above certain levels were ineligible for housing assistance. More and more, the people living in public housing were dependent families whose "minority status, lack of education or training, and/ or family conditions relegated them to housing of last resort" (Mitchell 1985, 195). Unemployment, high crime rates, delinquency, troubled schools, drug abuse, and dysfunctional families characterized public housing communities. Residents of surrounding areas viewed these conditions with alarm and feared a widening contagion. Pressure grew to seek alternative solutions to meet the housing needs of low-income people.

Critics of project-based housing believed that the private market could do the job of providing housing to needy families more efficiently and for less money than could the federal government. An alternative to public housing projects and low-income developments that policymakers had considered over the years was rent certificates given to households to use for housing in the private market (Frieden 1985; Mitchell 1985). One argument put forward in support of certificates was that privately owned units would be more decentralized and, it was believed, would offer better living conditions. A growing body of research argued that the neighborhood environment was critical in determining the life chances and experiences of people; housing projects and developments, with their concentration of poverty and the absence of positive role models, offered little support for social mobility. Thus, a "scattered-site approach—economic and social integration—[became] one of the major goals of all federal housing programs after the late 1960s" (Mitchell 1985, 198).

Legislation enacted in 1970 (U.S. House of Representatives 1970) laid the groundwork for the Experimental Housing Allowance Program (EHAP), which was launched in 1973 and provided housing allowances that could be used by families in housing of their own choice. EHAP was designed to test how tenant-based assistance (as opposed to project-based assistance) would work in practice.[3] This was followed by the Housing and Community Development Act of 1974's Section 8 Housing Certificate program (U.S. Senate 1974), which enabled participants to find and rent privately owned housing within the jurisdiction of the housing authority providing the assistance.

By the 1980s, HUD had added vouchers to the Section 8 program to expand tenant choice and to encourage the deconcentration of poor families. With a voucher, a family was free to choose any housing that complied with the requirements of the program and whose landlord or owner was willing to participate in the program. Legislation passed in 1991 further expanded the areas in which certificates and vouchers could be used.[4] Finally, in 1998, the programs were merged into a single program, the Housing Choice Voucher program (U.S. House of Representatives 1998); regulations took effect on October 1, 1999. The appendix provides additional details on the Housing Choice Voucher program.

Special Housing Mobility Programs

The Gautreaux housing program has received a great deal of positive publicity from advocates seeking to open up the suburbs to minority families. Its success provided the momentum for the Moving to Opportunity demonstration program, which is aimed at poverty rather than racial deconcentration.

The Gautreaux Program

The Gautreaux program was a response to a consent decree to a lawsuit filed against the Chicago Housing Authority (CHA) and HUD on behalf of public housing residents in Chicago (*Gautreaux v. Chicago Housing Authority* 1969). Administered by the nonprofit Leadership Council for Metropolitan Open Communities in Chicago, the program provided access to private-sector apartments either in mostly white suburbs or within the city of Chicago. Suburbs that were more than 30 percent black were excluded by the consent decree. Participants were assigned to city or suburban locations in a quasi-random manner. Under the Gautreaux program, placement counselors notified clients about available rental housing and the communities where the housing was located. They counseled clients about the advantages and the disadvantages of the moves, and they accompanied them on visits to the sites and the communities. To assure landlords that they would get good tenants and avoid problems like overcrowding, late rent payments, and vandalism, the program managers decided not to admit families with more than four children, large debts, or unacceptable housekeeping. As the program evolved, the council increasingly trained families to search for housing on their own (Rubinowitz and Rosenbaum 2000).

Between 1988 and 1992, an average of about 1,700 out of 2,000 families that signed up for the program were found eligible. However, only about one-fifth of this eligible group actually used their Section 8 certificates and moved. Self-selection (an unwillingness to be a pioneer in a predominantly white suburb) and housing availability (an inability to find a landlord who would rent a suitable unit to them before their certificate expired) explained most of the premove attrition (Rubinowitz and Rosenbaum 2000).

James Rosenbaum and colleagues used two survey data sets to evaluate the Gautreaux program: (1) interviews in 1982 with 114 suburban movers and 48 city movers, and follow-up interviews in 1989 with 68 of the original suburban movers and 39 original city movers, plus 10 new city-mover families[5]; and (2) a survey in 1988 with 230 suburban movers and 112 city movers. Analysis of these databases has produced an impressive set of papers, articles, reports, and a book (Rosenbaum 1991, 1993, 1995, 1998; Rosenbaum and DeLuca 2000; Rosenbaum, Reynolds, and DeLuca 2002; Rubinowitz and Rosenbaum 2000).

The analysis showed that (1) suburban movers were more likely to find jobs than those who moved within the city (but they did not necessarily obtain jobs with higher wages); and (2) the children of suburban movers dropped out of school less frequently and were more likely to go on to college. A key reason for the greater success of these suburban moves was the movers' feeling of safety. "Specifically, those who moved to high socio-economic status neighborhoods tended to feel safer, and their greater safety helped to explain the neighborhood effects on efficacy" (Rosenbaum, Reynolds, and DeLuca 2002, 72).

Despite the Gautreaux program's success and despite its being the largest housing mobility program in the country (7,100 participants received assistance, according to Housing Law Center 1997), it has had little or no impact on the degree of racial and poverty concentration in Chicago.[6] Furthermore, Gautreaux's positive results may not be generalizable to the larger Section 8 program because participants were self-selected (they volunteered to participate in the program), they were heavily screened, and the program was small in scale. A program including a more representative sample of low-income renters and without the above-described intensive screening and counseling procedures would be less likely to produce such positive results (Johnson, Ladd, and Ludwig 2002; Popkin, Buron, et al. 2000). Finally, the Gautreaux findings alone do not justify a shift toward a housing dispersal policy. "Similar benefits might occur by diversifying the economic mix of people moving into low-income neighborhoods (via economic development or mixed-income housing)" (Rosenbaum and DeLuca 2000, 6). Welfeld's (1998) realistic assessment of Gautreaux offered a balanced view of what could be expected if the program were replicated:

> The good news is that the Gautreaux program is replicable in other suburban areas. The bad news is that the process will be long and laborious and that the results will be so microscopic that it will take sophisticated and talented social scientists to uncover them. (p. 233)

Moving to Opportunity

The Moving to Opportunity demonstration, begun in the mid-1990s, is still being carried out in Baltimore, Boston, Chicago, Los Angeles, and New York City. By employing a more truly experimental design than the

Gautreaux program, it is attempting to obtain more conclusive evidence of neighborhood impacts by assigning families to one of three groups, using a lottery format. In the experimental group, families are required to move into areas with poverty rates of 10 percent or less, and they are provided with special counseling. Families assigned to the comparison group are provided with vouchers and are allowed to move into any neighborhood. The control group consists of families that are not provided with a voucher but are allowed to remain in public housing. Whereas the Gautreaux program focused on racial integration, MTO concentrates on income mixing (Goering et al. 1999; Goering and Feins 2003; Orr et al. 2003).

In 1996, HUD conducted an MTO grant competition and made eight small awards to groups of researchers with varied approaches and topics. Each team was given access to MTO participants at one of the five sites in order to evaluate various aspects of the families' early experiences there. Goering, Feins, and Richardson's (2002) cross-site analysis of the initial MTO demonstration program results indicate that, in general, the demonstration had a positive impact on the life chances of public housing residents from poor communities. That is, the "findings from single-site research studies show lower levels of fear, improved health outcomes, higher educational test scores, and lower rates of violent juvenile crime. There is no evidence, to date, of early effects on wages or employment" (p. 1). It should be noted that for some of the findings, both the comparison and experimental groups did better than the treatment group. Therefore, it is unclear how critical it is for voucher recipients to move to low-poverty neighborhoods and receive intensive counseling. Furthermore, it is unclear why MTO has failed to achieve improvements in employment like those in the Gautreaux program.

Rosenbaum and Harris's assertion (2001)—that the MTO program in Chicago "has achieved remarkable success in improving the neighborhood and housing conditions of participating families in the short term" (p. 342)—is questionable. After the move, statistically similar percentages of MTO and regular Section 8 respondents reported that their new neighborhood was better than their old one.[7]

MTO's positive impacts on children, based on the small grant studies, are of particular interest. Research teams in Boston (Katz, Kling, and Liebman 2001) and Baltimore (Ludwig, Ladd, and Duncan 2001) found that school-wide reading and math scores or pass rates were significantly higher in the treatment group children's schools, compared with the scores or rates of the control group children's schools. They also reported evidence of MTO having a positive impact on individual educational performance. Another Baltimore research team (Ludwig, Duncan, and Hirschfield 2001) found that juveniles in the treatment group had lower arrest rates for violent crime compared with juveniles in the control group; there were no significant differences, however, in the arrest rates for violent crime between juveniles in the treatment and comparison groups. Finally, there were insignificant differences in arrests for property crimes between those in the treatment and control groups.

In contrast to the empirical research carried out separately on MTO in the five cities, Popkin, Harris, and Cunningham's (2002) qualitative research draws from open-ended interviews with 58 adults and 39 children at all five MTO sites. Their research provides little evidence of neighborhood effects helping families achieve self-sufficiency. MTO movers did experience improvements in housing and neighborhood conditions, particularly with respect to personal safety, but so did regular Section 8 movers. Similarly, there was no evidence to indicate that MTO movers or their children were more likely than regular Section 8 movers to experience improvements in the social environment, in educational opportunities, or in economic opportunity. In general, the results highlighted the complexity of the movers' experiences. Many found it difficult to form meaningful social relationships in their new neighborhoods. Some of the children had problems of adjustment at their new schools (usually due to greater competition and higher standards), and parents chose to put the children back in schools near their public housing apartment.[8] Finally, it was impossible to accurately assess the impact on employment behavior for respondents in all groups, both because the economy was very strong in early 2001 and because of welfare reform.

The small grant research was followed by a more comprehensive and uniform assessment, carried out by Abt Associates Inc. and the National Bureau of Economic Research, which aimed to find the impact of the program at the midpoint of the 10-year research period originally mandated by Congress. The interim report of this effort, *Moving to Opportunity for Fair Housing Demonstration: Interim Impacts Evaluation* (Orr et al. 2003), offers mixed evidence regarding effectiveness. Although those in the experimental group achieved improved housing, neighborhood conditions, and safety, the demonstration had virtually no influence on any of the measures of educational attainment and virtually no impact on employment, earnings, or receipt of public assistance. It is important to recognize that improvements in employment and education might require more than the 4 to 7 years evaluated as part of the interim report. The final report—which will assess impacts 10 years after participants joined the program—may provide more conclusive results.

Policy experts differ sharply on the overall strengths of the MTO model. Wasserman (2001), summarizing results from HUD's small grants competition, notes that there was little evidence from MTO that moving to a more affluent neighborhood directly increased a family's self-sufficiency. She notes, however, that MTO may have an indirect effect on self-sufficiency. Those moving to more affluent neighborhoods were less likely to be exposed to crime, and their children were less likely to have been victims of crime. According to her, it is possible that less exposure to crime might lead to fewer problems "down the road"; parents may be able to focus on other things than keeping their children safe. The majority of parents who signed up for MTO said their main impetus for moving was to get away from gangs and drugs.

Johnson, Ladd, and Ludwig (2002) estimated that the dollar value to society from changes in teenage delinquency and children's educational outcomes was approximately $22,900 for those assigned to the MTO experimental group and $20,600 for those in the regular Section 8 group, implying that the MTO model is more cost-efficient than the regular Section voucher program because of the positive outcomes for the MTO children. Basgal and Villarreal (2001, 274) note, however, that (1) although intensive MTO-type counseling is needed in some areas like Chicago, it is not needed in others like Alameda County, California; (2) MTO counseling is expensive and without a massive infusion of funding to HUD, the cost of providing it would mean draconian reductions in the number of Section 8 recipients nationally; and (3) where the regular Section 8 program is effectively promoting wider locational choices, it would be more cost-efficient to expand the existing program rather than apply the expensive MTO model.[9] Furthermore, any attempt to compare the MTO model with the regular Section 8 program needs to take into account that in the former, individual householders must move to low-poverty neighborhoods. This requirement undercuts the foundation of housing vouchers, which is to expand housing choices.[10]

The Regular Section 8 Voucher Program

The previous section showed that special housing mobility programs (Gautreaux and MTO) have achieved some success in enabling lower-income families to relocate to better neighborhoods, and to a lesser degree, to progress toward self-sufficiency. The question is: Can the same goals be achieved for less cost, while allowing voucher recipients more choice under the regular operation of the Section 8 program? Results from studies of housing search and neighborhood outcomes under the regular Section 8 program, including research on the use of housing vouchers as part of HOPE VI public housing revitalization, show that the program has worked in some places but not others (for a discussion of the HOPE VI program, see Salama 1999).

Housing Search and Neighborhood Outcomes

Housing vouchers can lead to expanded choices only if voucher recipients are able to find landlords willing to rent to them. In recent years, voucher holders have experienced increased difficulty in finding housing where they can use their vouchers.[11] Across the United States, 31 percent of those holding Section 8 vouchers in 2001 were unable to find homes before the vouchers expired, up from 19 percent in 1993 (HUD and Harvard University's Joint Center for Housing Studies, cited in Kunkle 2002). A key factor explaining why families have difficulty using vouchers is the lack of housing of adequate quality at the right price (Finkel and Buron 2001; Sard 2001). In tight housing markets, many landlords are unwilling to rent to people with vouchers because they can charge higher rents to unsubsidized families.

Katz and Turner (2001) argue that the current fragmented system of administering housing assistance by multiple local housing authorities hinders the ability of families to move from the jurisdiction of one housing authority to that of another. The authors contend that Section 8 vouchers need to be administered regionally, with the agency chosen as a result of a competitive process. Alternatives to the currently fragmented system of administration would include state administration, a regional housing authority, nonprofit organizations, or for-profit providers. Basgal and Villarreal (2001) critique this proposal, noting (1) local housing authority administration is only a relatively minor factor in accounting for the lack of deconcentration of poverty (the concentration of affordable housing in particular areas is a more important cause); and (2) if Section 8 vouchers were administered regionally, then local concerns, like strict screening standards, would have to be dropped.

Popkin, Galster, and colleagues' (2000) baseline assessment of public housing desegregation cases shows that families seeking to make desegregative moves experience particular difficulty. In a dozen cases nationwide, HUD entered into consent agreements in which HUD, the local housing authority, and the local government agreed to implement specific remedy elements. HUD commissioned the Urban Institute to conduct research on the implementation of eight of these consent agreements originally entered into between 1987 and 1996. At all but two of the sites, some certificates or vouchers were issued with restrictions that required holders to use the subsidy in nonimpacted areas, defined as census tracts or blocks with a certain percentage of minority residents. Respondents seeking to move to low-minority areas had to overcome a number of barriers, including a fear of experiencing discrimination in predominantly white areas, a perception of a lack of affordable housing in nonimpacted areas, a lack of public transportation in suburban areas, and an unwillingness of landlords to accept Section 8 vouchers.

Movers' experiences with desegregative relocations were mixed. Some thought that their new units and communities were better, but others complained about poor housing and dangerous neighborhoods. Results for children were also mixed. Although some respondents spoke of positive school experiences, others reported a decline in school performance, attributing it to name calling and other prejudicial treatment received from students and the teacher. Desegregative moves had three types of impacts on the social integration of the movers: (1) some were fully accepted into the surrounding community; (2) others liked their neighborhood but were bothered by relatively minor problems, such as neighborhood gossiping and racial stereotyping; and (3) others kept themselves isolated and did not socialize with their neighbors. Many movers had weak ties to their current location and indicated that they would move if they could afford to do so.

Even with improved relocation counseling, an assessment of mobility counseling and services provided to participants in a Chicago mobility counseling program suggests that it will be difficult to increase the numbers of families making desegregative moves. In 1998, CHAC Inc., the private corporation that administers the voucher program in Chicago, created its own mobility program that used "a variety of methods—including individual counseling, life-skills training, landlord negotiation seminars, neighborhood tours and a security deposit loan assistance program—to foster moves to low-poverty, low-minority neighborhoods" (Cunningham et al. 2002, 2). The Urban Institute evaluated the mobility program's success using a three-wave panel survey of 203 voucher recipients. Most of those surveyed had participated in the CHAC mobility program, but some had moved with no assistance. After 12 months, about two-fifths had moved to an opportunity neighborhood. However, in contrast to what had been predicted, on measures of neighborhood quality (e.g., crime, social, and physical disorder), there were no significant differences between the responses from movers to low-poverty and high-poverty neighborhoods. These results may reflect the fact that there are considerable variations in neighborhood conditions within high-poverty census tracts. Consequently, by moving a few blocks, but remaining within a high-poverty area, householders can significantly improve their residential conditions.

In general, previous research offers mixed results on the ability of recipients of Section 8 housing vouchers as part of the regular program to improve their housing and neighborhood conditions. Goering, Stebbings, and Siewert (1995) note:

> Families receiving certificates and vouchers obtain housing in areas that are generally less poor and less segregated than the neighborhoods surrounding conventional projects. . . . [Nonetheless,] many Section 8 families continue to live in relatively segregated and economically distressed neighborhoods. (p. ii)

Several other studies have found that neighborhood conditions are better for the average Section 8 recipients than for public and assisted housing residents or unassisted renters, although not as good as for Section 8 recipients who receive special mobility assistance (Cunningham, Sylvester, and Turner 2000; Newman and Schnare 1997; Turner 1998).

A report by Quane, Rankin, and Joshi (2002) based on a survey of approximately 2,400 low-income families living in poor and near-poor neighborhoods in Boston, Chicago, and San Antonio provides additional evidence that the Section 8 voucher program does not always help families move to better neighborhoods. Although families with housing assistance—either public housing or a Section 8 voucher—usually had a smaller housing cost burden, they tended to live in some of the most disadvantaged areas of the city, where they were more likely to encounter major problems with crime, vandalism, and unsupervised children. These families were also more likely to distrust their neighbors and said that they would move provided they had the means to relocate.[12]

Whereas the Gautreaux and MTO programs involved voluntary approaches to deconcentration, the *Hollman v. Cisneros* lawsuit (1998) in the Minneapolis–Saint Paul metropolitan area gave Edward Goetz (2002, 2003) an opportunity to test both voluntary and involuntary approaches to deconcentration within the same community.[13] Goetz interviewed more than 600 households in the Twin Cities, divided into treatment and comparison groups. The treatment groups consisted of (1) residents who had been involuntarily displaced from public housing because of demolition, (2) families that had voluntarily moved into replacement units, and (3) families that had voluntarily used mobility certificates. For the statistical analysis, the second and third treatment groups were combined. The two comparison groups were participants in the city's regular Section 8 program and "stay-at-home" public housing residents. Goetz's "program hypothesis" was that families involved in the deconcentration program would report improvements in their living conditions relative to their previous places of residence and relative to control groups. His "method hypothesis" was that involuntarily displaced families would report fewer improvements in living conditions and more problems in relocation compared to voluntarily mobile families.

Goetz's results provide less support for the deconcentration hypothesis than has been reported for MTO, Gautreaux, or other special housing mobility programs. Evidence for the benefits of moves to low-poverty areas was greatest on issues of public safety and neighborhood civility, but there was little evidence of improvement with regard to neighborhood satisfaction and employment. The study provided partial support for the method hypothesis. For example, taken together, "the findings suggest that the involuntary group respondents consider their children to be more socially isolated after their relocation than do those who voluntarily relocated" (Goetz 2002, 114).

Goetz asserts that one possible explanation for the lack of program effects in his study vis-à-vis earlier ones (e.g., Gautreaux, MTO) is that most earlier studies were limited to families who participated voluntarily. This suggests a selection bias in earlier research. "Inclusion of involuntary

participants is bound to reduce the level and scope of program effects"
(Goetz 2002, 121).[14]

The fact that dispersed families in Goetz's study were not likely to
achieve increases in social interaction with neighbors may be interpreted
positively in that these families might have been predicted to become more
socially isolated. Conversely, the results indicate the need "for caution related to the ability of deconcentrated families to integrate into new environments" (Goetz 2002, 122). The relative lack of interaction might, for
example, mean that it is difficult for lower-income householders to con-
nect with their middle-class neighbors and learn about new job opportunities.

Because it focuses on severely distressed developments, the HOPE
VI program affects some of the nation's most disadvantaged families, including many single-headed households with children. Consequently, some
of these families have experienced serious obstacles in relocating.

Buron and colleagues' 2000 study has been the largest and most sys-
tematic study of outcomes for HOPE VI participants. On the basis of a
retrospective survey of former residents from eight HOPE VI sites where
redevelopment activities began between 1993 and 1998, the authors found
that most respondents experienced improvements in housing conditions
at their new site as compared with their original distressed public housing. However, a substantial proportion of those who received vouchers or
who transferred to another public housing development reported problems with crime or drug trafficking in their new neighborhood. Kingsley,
Johnson, and Pettit's 2000 analysis of HUD administrative data for former
residents at 73 HOPE VI sites in 48 cities indicated that the majority of
those who received vouchers had moved to neighborhoods with lower-
poverty rates than those of their original HOPE VI developments.

Popkin and colleagues' 1998 assessment of the revitalization of the
Henry Horner Homes in Chicago, published in 2000 (Popkin, Gwiasda,
et al. 2000), indicated that many of the former residents might not benefit from the revitalization in the long term. Relatively few of the original
residents tried to move back to the development. Many had been declared
ineligible or relocated on their own without assistance. Popkin,
Cunningham, and colleagues' (2002) *CHA Relocation Counseling Assessment*
supports this pessimistic conclusion. A sample of 190 residents was tracked
through the relocation process. After one year, only two-fifths had moved
to a housing unit in the private market. Those who did move experienced

improvements in housing conditions and neighborhood safety, even though the areas to which they moved had high poverty rates and high levels of racial segregation. However, the majority faced obstacles, such as lack of experience with private-market housing and serious personal problems—substance abuse, depression, domestic violence, and gang affiliation—that made it difficult for them to search effectively for housing and made them less attractive to landlords. (See Popkin and Cunningham 2000 for a review of the literature on what is known about barriers and opportunities to renting housing in the Chicago area.)

Smith's 2002 study used focus groups and administrative interviews to examine how relocatees at four HOPE VI sites (Baltimore, Louisville, San Antonio, and Seattle) made choices about replacement housing. The perceived availability of housing and time constraints were the two main influences on housing choice. Many feared moving to unfamiliar areas, and some reported encountering discrimination or difficulty finding affordable housing units.

Reclustering and Neighborhood Spillover Effects

Although HUD has encouraged low-income families to relocate to low-income and low-poverty neighborhoods, often this goal has not been achieved. Many Section 8 voucher recipients make short-distance moves, often to areas of concentrated poverty with high proportions of minorities or to fragile neighborhoods experiencing racial change (Goetz 2002, 2003; Hartung and Henig 1997; Khadduri 2001; McClure 2001; Popkin and Cunningham 2000). These are precisely the areas where landlords are most willing to rent to Section 8 voucher recipients.[15] Because of reclustering in particular communities, many residents, civic leaders, and politicians have expressed concern "that clusters of Section 8 households can destabilize neighborhoods, bringing drugs, crime, and antisocial behavior and precipitating a cycle of neighborhood disinvestment and decline" (Turner, Popkin, and Cunningham 2000, 9).

National research on the Section 8 program suggests that clustering is not a widespread problem. Devine and colleagues' 2003 report using September 2000 data from HUD's Multifamily Tenant Characteristics System (MTCS) indicates that in most neighborhoods, housing vouchers are used in only a small fraction of the total occupied housing stock. "For example, in almost 90 percent of all neighborhoods with voucher units, the program represents less than five percent of the housing stock. . . . In just under three percent of the neighborhoods where the program is found, housing vouchers utilize at least 10 percent of the housing stock" (p. 9). Similarly, Kingsley, Johnson, and Pettit's 2000 analysis of HUD administrative data indicated that clustering—large numbers of relocated households living in the same census tracts—occurred at only a few sites.

Where clustering does occur—in cities like Baltimore (Smith 2002) and Chicago (Fischer 1999; Husock 2000)—it is widely perceived as a problem. For example, Smith (2002) notes that at HOPE VI sites in Baltimore, Louisville, San Antonio, and Seattle, voucher recipients were aware of and concerned about the perceived and actual impact of large numbers of other housing voucher recipients moving into their new neighborhood.

Recent empirical research indicates that these concerns about voucher clustering are often realistic. Galster, Tatian, and Smith's 1999 Baltimore County, Maryland, study found that "vulnerable" lower-income neighborhoods experienced lower property values as a result of close proximity to Section 8 units. Similarly, Galster and colleagues found through focus groups that residents of vulnerable neighborhoods were more likely to be concerned about negative neighborhood impacts. Lee, Culhane, and Wachter (1999), in a Philadelphia study, found that Section 8 certificates or vouchers were associated with lower property values. Magazine and newspaper articles in a variety of cities, including Baltimore (Olesker 1996; Swope 2002) and Cincinnati (Alltucker 2002; Thompson 2002), describe negative community impacts (crime, vandalism, housing deterioration) resulting from the in-migration of large numbers of Section 8 families to particular communities.

Turner, Popkin, and Cunningham (2000) offer a balanced and cautious assessment of negative neighborhood impacts resulting from Section 8 reclustering.

> There is no evidence to indicate that the Section 8 program is undermining the health of large numbers of urban neighborhoods. Although significant levels of geographic clustering do appear to occur, neighborhood opposition to the program has been limited to a relatively small number of loudly publicized instances. Nevertheless, the potential for adverse neighborhood impacts should not be ignored. The flare-ups of neighborhood opposition that have occurred may be symptoms of serious problems of program implementation and have the potential to undermine support for the Section 8 program as a whole. (p. 11)[16]

The literature offers three suggestions for dealing with reclustering when it occurs. First, in the case of the vouchering out of HOPE VI developments, public housing authorities may need to screen out families that are unprepared to move into private housing. These families may require transitional housing and intensive social services (Popkin 2002; Popkin, Levy, et al. 2002). Second, existing landlord training programs aimed at keeping drug dealing and other forms of illegal activities off private rental properties ought to be expanded.[17] Third, public housing authorities need to develop analytical tools "to distinguish the truly fragile neighborhoods and manage their programs in a way that discourages families from moving to those neighborhoods without imposing an out-and-out prohibition" (Khadduri 2001, 77).

In general, the existing research on Section 8 vouchers yields somewhat mixed results on how families fare after relocation. Many that have received vouchers are living in better housing in at least somewhat better neighborhoods. Simultaneously, some (especially those relocated due to HOPE VI demolitions) continue to reside in areas that are still very poor and that are crime ridden. The Chicago HOPE VI research implies that the subgroup of residents that had the most complex personal problems are having difficulty making the transition to either private housing or revitalized HOPE VI developments. The reclustering of Section 8 voucher holders is a problem, but only in a small number of places.

Reexamining Neighborhood Effects

Current interest in housing vouchers and housing mobility programs is based on the assumption that the characteristics of one's surrounding neighborhood (e.g., the degree of accessibility to jobs, the extent of income mixing) can affect a family's ability to achieve self-sufficiency. However, a growing number of social scientists are skeptical about the significance of these neighborhood effects.

Khadduri (2001) notes that although there has been widespread interest in income mixing, inadequate attention has been given to the practical problems of implementation. To what sort of neighborhoods should voucher families move? What does the term "income diversity" mean within a housing development? Should the definition of neighborhood quality take into account race as well as income? Would it be better to use a measure of income diversity rather than the level of poverty to measure income mixing? Would it be preferable to set incremental goals for families—that is, to move to areas with lower poverty rates—than to move to low-poverty areas?

In contrast to what is generally assumed to be true, housing mobility programs may not necessarily promote access to jobs. Macek, Khattak, and Quercia (2001; cited in Jennings and Quercia 2001) assert that decades of research on the spatial mismatch are inconclusive. The employment prospects of voucher holders may not really improve with moves to the suburbs, because they would have less access to public transit as well as no access to an auto (Basgal and Villarreal 2001).

Recent case studies also provide little concrete evidence of any benefits of social mixing. In the Rosenbaum, Stroh, and Flynn 1996 case study of Lake Parc Place (Chicago), very low- and higher-income tenants interacted, but these relationships were not intensive enough to promote social learning; employment rates for both groups actually declined the first year. Brophy and Smith's 1997 case studies of mixed-income developments showed little interaction between low- and higher-income residents,[18] and no discernible impact on the employment of lower-income residents. Schwartz and Tajbakhsh (2001) compared mixed-income developments in the Bronx, New York City; Chicago; Massachusetts; and California. They found little evidence that social mixing had any direct positive impacts through social interaction and/or social networks. "There is no real evidence that mixed-income housing is a remedy for social ills," they reported, adding that policymakers and researchers ought to view these developments with "diminished expectations" (p. 27). They do point out, however, that social mixing may have an indirect positive impact. "For poorer households, living in a residential environment that is safe and dependable may provide the stepping stone they require to enter and remain in the job market" (p. 29).

Kleit's analysis of survey data from scattered-site and clustered public housing residents in Montgomery County, Maryland, undercuts the argument that moving to low-poverty neighborhoods provides lower-income households with greater access to social capital (Kleit 2001a, 2001b, 2002).[19] Kleit found (1) dispersed scattered-site public housing residents were not more likely than clustered residents to rely on their social ties to neighbors to find out about jobs, (2) dispersed residents lacked close social ties to their middle-income neighbors,[20] and (3) dispersed residents sought better jobs as measured by occupational prestige scores. Kleit speculates why dispersed residents conducted more effective job searches. "Dispersed residents are forced to reach beyond their local neighborhood to find new social resources . . . which provide them with increased access to a broader array of opportunities" (2002, 97). Future research is needed on whether low-income residents of low-poverty neighborhoods do, in fact, go out of the local neighborhood to take advantage of employment opportunities, and if they do, how they utilize these opportunities.

America's mobility-oriented approach has not yet been adopted in Europe. In part, this is due to the fact that in many European countries, the socially rented sector (i.e., housing operated by local government or by nonprofit groups) is much larger than the privately rented sector. Therefore, large-scale movement from the former to the latter would not be feasible. Furthermore, the notion that the life chances of the poor are additionally disadvantaged by residing in a poor neighborhood is not as widely accepted in Europe as in the United States (Kearns 2002; Whitehead 2002).

There has also been far less research on social mixing in Europe than in the United States, but the limited European research does not support the presumed benefits of mixing. Musterd's (2002) Amsterdam study refuted the notion that the social composition of an area influences opportunities:

> Among the findings was that for those who had a weak social position in 1989 (whether in poverty), the social composition of the environment (percentage of the population receiving social benefits) had hardly any effect on their social position in 1994. (Musterd 2002, 142)

Atkinson and Kintrea (1999) studied social patterns on four council housing estates in Scotland, conducting open-ended interviews of owners and renters and using diaries that the owners and renters had kept to document their experiences. The researchers found that the introduction of owners into communities that had been exclusively rental did not change social patterns. "Their lives [those of owners and renters] are quite different, and mutual residence by itself does not bring them together" (p. 50). Nor was there any evidence that the presence of owners affected the views and attitudes of the renters or their families.

Why have existing mixed-income and mixed-tenure programs produced such disappointing results? Heather MacDonald (1997) sees family values and moral character as the root cause of urban poverty. "While a lawless, chaotic neighborhood unquestionably poses great risks to a child's moral development, a strong family can act as a powerful buffer" (p. 756). Thus, in her view, for an urban policy to have any chance for success, it would be necessary to reconstruct the urban family, that is, increase the number of stable, supportive families. "Put[ting] inner-city residents close to middle- and upper-class citizens and hop[ing] that some values rub off . . . is a highly inefficient way to build character" (p. 761).

Conclusions

The literature review suggests that by facilitating moves to low-poverty, low-minority neighborhoods, special mobility programs (e.g., Gautreaux and MTO) have succeeded in helping families move to safer neighborhoods, with better schools than their children had attended in the inner city. But it must be stated that the lack of research on the long-term effects on children, such as future improvements in their employment circumstances due to better educational attainment, makes it impossible to offer conclusive assessments on the connection between these two programs and social mobility.

It is unlikely, however, that these two special programs will be expanded to serve the entire Section 8 voucher population.[21] First, although intensive counseling might be desirable, it would be extremely expensive to provide such help to all Section 8 voucher recipients. Second, it would be unwise to require all (or most) voucher holders to move to low-poverty areas. Such a requirement would contradict a fundamental aim of the voucher program: to promote free choice. Many voucher recipients want to remain in the central city, close to their friends and relatives, near community and religious services, and in close proximity to public transit. Third, it may not be feasible to apply an MTO-type model to the segment of the urban poor that has physical and mental problems, criminal records, and histories of domestic violence, substance abuse, or poor credit or housekeeping histories. This segment of the poor population needs transitional or supportive housing and other forms of social assistance (Popkin, Buron, et al. 2000; Popkin, Gwiasda, et al. 2000; Popkin 2002; Popkin, Cunningham, and Woodley 2003).[22] A massive effort to relocate all the poor to the suburbs—including drug dealers, criminals, and those who engage in antisocial behavior—could destabilize working-class and middle-class communities, especially those that are already vulnerable to racial and income change (MacDonald 1997).

As an alternative to a national MTO-type program, it may be desirable in some places to rely on the regular Section 8 voucher program to widen locational choices. However, most of the research that has been conducted has highlighted the difficulty that many voucher recipients experience in carrying out their housing search and in relocating to better neighborhoods. It is important to note that much of this latter research was carried out in Chicago, where voucher recipients were former public housing residents who were relocated from deteriorating public housing and had great difficulty finding housing. What is not adequately recognized is that there may be places where the program works well for many of the urban poor and where, because of good management, the program does not adversely affect the communities to which voucher holders relocate. More research is needed to better explain variations in the effectiveness of the Section 8 program in different places. The present book is addressed to this gap in the existing research.

Notes

1. There are two ways to deconcentrate poverty: (1) through the dispersal of low-income families using housing vouchers or scattered-site subsidized private and/or public housing; and (2) by creating mixed-income developments in the inner city. Although this chapter focuses on the housing voucher research literature, we will also discuss relevant research on income mixing in public housing and publicly subsidized private developments.

2. It is important to recognize that tenant-based subsidies are only one part of a comprehensive strategy to cure segregation and to mitigate the high costs of residential segregation. Curative strategies include inclusionary housing (e.g., the Montgomery County, Maryland, Moderately Priced Dwelling Unit program; see Maryland–National Capitol Park and Planning Commission n.d.), fair share housing policies, fair housing enforcement, scattered-site public housing, and community development, including mixed-income development, to attract diverse in-movers. Mitigating strategies include school desegregation by mandatory busing or magnet schools, fiscal reform to equalize public services across municipal boundaries, reverse commuting to jobs, and regional workforce development alliances or networks (Briggs 2003).

3. See Solomon and Fenton (1973) for an analysis of the EHAP demonstration in Kansas City.

4. Feins et al. (1997) review the history of the Section 8 certificate and voucher programs.

5. In the 1982 survey, when talking about their children, interviewees were asked to concentrate on the experiences of one randomly selected child who was between 6 and 17 years of age and had lived and attended school in both an inner-city neighborhood and a suburban community.

6. Squires (2002) notes that although the limited size of the Gautreaux program made it less threatening and controversial, this same feature reduced its impact on the segregated nature of Chicago's housing market. The index of black–white segregation in Chicago was hardly affected, declining just 6 points over 20 years—from 91.9 in 1970 to 85.8 in 1990 (p. 371). Furthermore, it is unlikely that this modest decline in segregation was due to Gautreaux. Other cities lacking this special program experienced similar declines.

7. Furthermore, the results of a logistic regression analysis indicated that being in MTO did not significantly increase the likelihood of being in the labor force or being employed.

8. In general, the early MTO results provide a much less rosy picture of the benefits of moving on employment and educational opportunities than was true for the Gautreaux program.

9. Basgal and Villarreal (2001) estimate that the average public housing authority could help 60 clients under the regular Section 8 program for what it would cost to successfully counsel one family under MTO. This figure is arrived at by dividing $3,077, the average counseling cost to help an MTO family find a unit, by $50.92, the average monthly administrative fee the PHAs receive from the U.S. Department of Housing and Urban Development (HUD). Basgal and Villarreal assume that a PHA uses one month's administrative fee to fund all initial costs associated with a family, including landlord outreach, counseling, income screening and verification, unit inspection, and so forth.

10. Rosenbaum and DeLuca (2000) concede a key point to MTO skeptics when they acknowledge that the MTO model undercuts individual choice. "Some policy makers support the idea that families should be able to choose new neighborhoods for whatever reasons are most salient to them (e.g., proximity to friends and families, etc.), even though those choices may not result in a move to a low-poverty neighborhood" (p. 341).

11. This section draws heavily from Popkin, Levy, et al.'s (2002) *HOPE VI Panel Study: Baseline Report*.

12. One would presume that Section 8 voucher recipients would experience better housing and neighborhood conditions than families living in public housing. Unfortunately, Quane, Rankin, and Joshi (2002) did not provide separate results for voucher recipients and public housing residents.

13. The consent decree resulted in the demolition of more than 700 units of public housing on the near north side of Minneapolis, mandated the development of more than 700 units of scattered-site replacement housing in

nonconcentrated parts of the city, and made 900 Section 8 vouchers available to families willing to move to low-poverty areas.

14. Similarly, families in the Robert Taylor homes that were involuntarily relocated by the Chicago Housing Authority when their homes were scheduled for demolition experienced little change in neighborhood conditions (Johnson, Ladd, and Ludwig 2002).

15. Landlords can choose whether or not to participate in the Section 8 voucher program. They can also rent to a small number of Section 8 families and then later choose not to rent to any more voucher recipients. In general, landlords in the more sought-after suburbs choose not to participate in the program, whereas some landlords in the inner city depend on the Section 8 program to fill their units. Often, as part of the Section 8 briefing session, voucher holders are provided with lists of landlords interested in renting to Section 8 families. All the above factors help to account for the clustering of Section 8 families in high-poverty, high-minority, inner-city neighborhoods.

16. Freeman and Botein (2002) and HUD (2000) also offer balanced assessments of the reclustering issue.

17. A private consultant (Campbell DeLong Resources Inc. 1998), using U.S. Department of Justice funding, has developed a landlord training course and manual aimed at low-income rental landlords, which includes but is not limited to those renting to Section 8 voucher holders. The first training program was held in Portland, Oregon, in 1989, and since then, jurisdictions in many states have presented the program in their own communities. "The Landlord Training Program teaches rental owners and managers how to keep drug activity off their property. . . . It teaches them their responsibility as landlords in working with police and neighbors to keep drug and other illegal activity out of their rental properties" (pp. I-2 to I-3). The course content includes applicant screening, rental agreements (approaches to strengthen the ability to evict drug-dealing tenants), and Section 8 housing (differences in the responsibilities of landlords and tenants in Section 8 compared with typical rental housing).

18. At several sites, the low-income population consisted of families with children; the higher-income population consisted of childless households, such as graduate students. These differences made social interaction unlikely.

19. Poor households living in scattered-site housing may be seen as roughly comparable to housing voucher recipients moving into low-poverty areas.

20. The absence of such meaningful ties should not be surprising in terms of contact theory; the superficial ties may simply reflect disparities in social status.

21. Nevertheless, Galster (2002) has offered the following support for such a proposal: "Expansion of tenant-based mobility programs along the lines of MTO can be justified in the U.S. on grounds of social costs and benefits, based on the evidence at hand" (pp. 7–8).

22. Obviously, an expanded regular Section 8 housing voucher program would not meet these families' needs either. Our point is that any poverty

deconcentration strategy alone would be inappropriate for this poverty subgroup. If the Section 8 housing voucher program is expanded, as we argue in this book, it would need to be accompanied by an expansion in supportive and transitional housing.

2

Vouchering Out Distressed Subsidized Developments

During the 1990s, the Office of Property Disposition in the U.S. Department of Housing and Urban Development (HUD) began closing a number of severely distressed federally subsidized properties that had been privately owned until they were taken over by HUD through foreclosure. The tenants who were forced to move out of these properties were given vouchers that they could use for the housing of their choice. No restrictions were placed on where residents could relocate, nor was mobility counseling emphasized. In most cases, tenants were offered moderate counseling—that is, counseling more intensive than the counseling usually provided to Section 8 participants,[1] but less intensive than that provided in the Moving to Opportunity for Fair Housing Demonstration (MTO) or Gautreaux programs. The disposition of these properties—or their "vouchering out"—provided HUD with the opportunity to gain insight into the housing and neighborhood outcomes for households receiving vouchers in the context of a program that had no relocation requirements. Where would families move? Would moderate counseling lead to more effective searches? What

Portions of this chapter are adapted from David P. Varady, Carole C. Walker, and Xinhao Wang, "Voucher Recipient Achievement of Improved Housing Conditions in the U.S.: Do Moving Distance and Relocation Services Matter?" In *Urban Studies* 38, 8: 1273–1304. ©2001 Carfax Publishing/Taylor & Francis. www.tandf.co.uk/journals/carfax/00420980.html

Portions of this chapter are adapted from David P. Varady and Carole C. Walker, "Vouchering Out Distressed Subsidized Developments: Does Moving Lead to Improvements in Housing and Neighborhood Conditions?" In *Housing Policy Debate* 11, 1: 115–162. ©2000 Fannie Mae Foundation, Washington, D.C. Used with permission.

difficulties would families encounter in the search process? How would
the quality of the new housing units and neighborhoods compare with the
old, and how satisfied would families be with their new surroundings?

To answer these questions, HUD funded a study to examine the experiences of households relocated from a number of properties. The research was conducted by the Center for Urban Policy Research (CUPR)
at Rutgers University between 1995 and 1997 (Varady and Walker 1998).
The main objective of the research was to determine the housing and
neighborhood outcomes for families that had received vouchers to leave
their homes in assisted housing for residence in unassisted housing.

In building upon the HUD study, this chapter addresses a key limi-
tation of existing housing voucher research: an overreliance on two of the
special mobility programs, the Gautreaux and the MTO programs. Although the two programs have produced promising results in improved
neighborhood conditions—and in the case of Gautreaux, higher employment rates and higher levels of educational achievement for the children—
these are voluntary programs that draw the most motivated householders.
Less selective programs might achieve less impressive results. Furthermore,
the two programs have three features that distinguish them from the regular Section 8 program: (1) intensive relocation counseling, (2) geographical restrictions on where families can move, and (3) the screening out of
multiproblem families that might create troubles for neighbors.

Edward Goetz (2003), drawing on his research on the *Hollman v.
Cisneros* Minneapolis desegregation litigation, is openly skeptical of the
generalizability of the Gautreaux and MTO findings to voucher recipients nationally. Goetz found that, in general, the Hollman participants did
not fare as well as participants in the Gautreaux and MTO programs. This
is likely due to the fact that the Hollman participants included both involuntary and voluntary movers, and the involuntary movers reported fewer
benefits than the voluntary ones.[2] Many who did not want to relocate experienced postmove problems. Furthermore, they tended to move to areas
of concentrated poverty and to areas that were becoming poorer and home
to a greater proportion of minority residents over time.

The research on the vouchered-out developments presented in this
chapter extends Goetz's research in Minneapolis. Whereas he focused on
families displaced from public housing, we focus on families displaced from
federally subsidized private developments. Although privately owned, these
severely distressed developments had fallen prey to the same kind of woeful

conditions afflicting the worst public housing projects. Our working hypotheses, based on Goetz's research, were that (1) the families would make short-distance moves; (2) disproportionately large numbers would be dissatisfied with their home and neighborhood;[3] (3) most would report little or no improvement in residential conditions;[4] and (4) those that made long-distance moves and took advantage of relocation counseling would be the most likely to be satisfied with their new home, whereas those that were reluctant to move in the first place would be the least likely to be satisfied.

We found mixed support for these hypotheses. Although many of the vouchered-out residents chose to remain in the same area as their old developments, most reported that they were satisfied with their new home and neighborhood, and most said that their residential conditions had improved. As predicted, those who were reluctant to move were, in fact, less likely to be satisfied with their new home. However, in contrast to what had been anticipated, the utilization of relocation counseling had little impact on satisfaction, and those families that made longer-distance moves were not more likely to be satisfied with their new home than those that remained near their old developments.

These results indicate that it may be unrealistic to expect most low-income families that are given vouchers as part of relocation from distressed public or private housing to move to new or unfamiliar neighborhoods without intensive counseling and/or requirements as to where they can move. However, if the goal of the effort is to improve residential conditions, providing families with a voucher may be all that many of them require.

Research Strategy and Methods

The vouchering-out study employed a multiple-case embedded case study design (Yin 1994). The research design called for case studies of four vouchered-out properties. At each site, an individual case study was undertaken as a complete investigation, in which a variety of evidence and data was collected to determine the facts and arrive at the conclusions of the case. The focus in each case study was to determine the implementation and outcomes of the vouchering-out process. Data sources included a survey of residents, key informant interviews, windshield surveys, HUD documents and published materials, and a geographic information system (GIS) analysis of neighborhood outcomes. Following data collection, the results for the four case studies were compared and combined to arrive at overall findings for the vouchering-out program.

A primary data source was a telephone survey of former residents of the developments. Two hundred and one vouchered-out householders from the four sites were interviewed by telephone during November and December 1996.[5] The survey included open-ended as well as closed-ended questions and covered premove housing, the housing search, counseling, the voucher experience, current housing and neighborhood conditions (including safety), and household demographic characteristics. (For additional information on the survey, see Varady and Walker 1998.)

To measure the use of counseling services, we first asked respondents whether they were aware of the existence of relocation counseling services and, if so, whether they used this counseling to find a new home. We created an index to measure the use/nonuse of relocation services by cross-tabulating the use of counseling services by awareness of counseling. Respondents fell into one of three groups: 30 percent were unaware of the existence of relocation counseling; 31 percent were aware of these services, but had not used them; and the remaining 39 percent had used one or more of these services.

Respondents who had used relocation counseling were asked whether they had received 1 or more of 13 possible types of help. Seven of the services were used by more than half the tenants: help in paying for moving expenses (76 percent); help in understanding fair housing laws (76 percent); help in calculating what tenants could afford to pay in rent (72 percent); listings of housing vacancies (67 percent); help in understanding lease agreements (57 percent); help in filling out HUD applications (57 percent); and help in choosing neighborhoods (54 percent). Four other services were used by fewer than half the tenants: transportation to view available housing (45 percent); counseling on managing the family budget (44 percent); help in completing rental applications (43 percent); assistance in setting up utility accounts (32 percent); and dealing with family problems (17 percent). On average, residents used 6.7 of the services.

Principal components analysis applied to the 13 counseling questions yielded a four-component solution (table 2.1). The four factors were grouped together as (1) help with forms, (2) help in dealing with landlords, (3) help in budgeting, and (4) help in the housing search.[6] Sum-

TABLE 2.1

Rotated Component Matrix, Relocation Counseling Services

	Component			
	1	*2*	*3*	*4*
				Housing
Type of Help	*Forms*	*Landlords*	*Budgets*	*Search*
Listing possible places to call upon	0.133	0.163	0.032	0.870*
Deciding the neighborhood to search in	0.032	−0.034	0.508	0.459*
Calculating how much you could afford to pay for rent	0.215	0.024	0.580*	0.390
Managing your household budget	0.008	0.024	0.852*	0.012
Dealing with family problems	0.541*	0.307	0.197	−0.261
Filling out applications for HUD	0.746*	−0.046	−0.057	0.082
Filling out rental applications and references	0.648*	0.083	0.377	0.027
Understanding lease or rental agreements	0.172	0.895*	0.096	0.118
Setting up accounts with utility companies	0.595*	0.152	0.142	0.184
Arranging for transportation to possible rental locations	0.596*	−0.039	0.197	0.316
Paying for moving expenses	0.498*	0.360	−0.205	−0.101
Understanding fair housing laws	0.301	0.267	0.499*	−0.161
Dealing with neighborhood or landlord problems after the move	0.014	0.933*	0.044	0.068

Note: Numbers with asterisks are for questions loading highest on that component. These items were included in the summated scale for the factor listed on the top of the column. "Deciding the neighborhood to search in" was assigned to the housing search factor because it loaded relatively highly and because it fit more logically into that dimension.

mated scales were prepared for each of the four factors by adding up the number of services within that category that were utilized by the respondent. For example, the first scale (help with forms) was based on six items; scale scores ranged from 0 to 6. These four factors were included in the regression analysis discussed later in this chapter.

Informant interviews provided a second key data source. Interviews with housing officials, relocation counselors, landlords, and others in each of the cities were conducted in person or by telephone. These were tape-recorded, transcribed, and computer-analyzed using the NUD.IST qualitative analysis package. Third, neighborhood windshield survey worksheets were completed by the research team and compared with survey worksheets completed by the local planning department staffs. These surveys were used to assess housing and neighborhood physical conditions in pre- and postmove neighborhoods. Fourth, published materials and other documents at the four sites were gathered and reviewed. These included HUD documents and reports, land-use maps, census data, and newspaper articles.

Finally, a GIS analysis assessed neighborhood outcomes for the voucher recipients. A database was assembled to link the spatial coordinates of each household's destination to the socioeconomic characteristics of the surrounding neighborhood (indicated by median housing value, median household income, and percentage black population). The analysis measured the distance moved by voucher recipients, compared the socioeconomic characteristics of the new and old neighborhoods, and examined the relationship between the distance moved by voucher recipients and the characteristics of the new neighborhood. The results of this analysis were incorporated into the case studies.

In 1999, after the HUD report had been completed, we geocoded the addresses of the 201 survey respondents; we were successful in matching 182 cases. We used the geocoded addresses to create a data file containing the respondent identification number, the distance moved, and four neighborhood socioeconomic characteristics based on the census tract block group in which the household lived (median income, median housing value, proportion owner-occupied, proportion black). Next, using the identification number as the common variable, we created a merged file comprising the geographic file and the survey file. The merged file was used for the multivariate analysis for this chapter. Table 2.2 defines the variables included in the analysis and provides descriptive information with respect to these factors. Tables 2.3 and 2.4 report the results of the regression analysis dealing with the impact of different background characteristics on components of the housing search and the level of housing satisfaction.[7]

The regression results were used to prepare path diagrams (not included here for space reasons) portraying the direct impacts of background characteristics on housing satisfaction and the indirect impacts through features of the housing search.[8] Tables 2.5 and 2.6 summarize the indirect, direct, and total effects of background characteristics.

The Vouchering Out of Federally Subsidized Properties

At the time of the study, HUD was vouchering out nearly two dozen federally subsidized properties that had run into trouble. The properties were

TABLE 2.2

Descriptive Information for Variables Included in the Regression Analysis

Variable	Definition	Mean
Background demographic characteristics		
Age	Actual age of household head. Results ranged from 20 to 88.	40.88
Children	Number of children at home: (1) none, (2) one, (3) two, (4) three or more.	2.37
Married	Married: (0) no (1) yes.	0.08
Divorced	Divorced: (0) no (1) yes.	0.11
Separated	Separated: (0) no (1) yes.	0.16
Never married	Never married: (0) no (1) yes. Widowed was the reference category.	0.52
Income	Total family income: (1) below $5,000, (2) $5,000–$9,999, (3) $10,000–$14,999, (4) $15,000 and over.	1.94
Education	Highest grade completed: (1) less than high school, (2) high school degree, (3) more than high school degree.	1.88
Employed, current location	Employed at current location: (0) no (1) yes.	0.36
Unemployed, current location	Unemployed at current location: (0) no (1) yes.	0.23
Not looking for work, current location	Not looking for work at current location: (0) no (1) yes. Retired was the reference category.	0.32
Public assistance	Whether reported receiving any type of public assistance (AFDC, general assistance, SSI) on one or more of three questions dealing with current income sources.	0.7
Employed, previous location	Employed at previous location: (0) no (1) yes.	0.31
Unemployed, previous location	Unemployed at previous location: (0) no (1) yes.	0.24
Did not look for work, previous location	Did not look for work at previous location (0) no (1) yes. Retired was the reference category.	0.35
Background housing characteristics		
Crowding, current location	Ratio of people to rooms, postmove. Results ranged from 0.11 to 1.20.	0.5
Rental burden, current location	Ratio of monthly rent to total household monthly income. Results ranged from 0.00 to 0.96.	0.18
Crowding, previous location	Ratio of people to persons, pre-move. Results ranged from 0.17 to 1.20.	0.55
House	New home is a house (0) no (1) yes.	0.43

(continued)

TABLE 2.2 (continued)

Variable	Definition	Mean
Background locational characteristics		
Eutaw Gardens	Lived in Eutaw Gardens, Baltimore: (0) no (1) yes.	0.27
Woodsong	Lived in Woodsong, Newport News, Virginia: (0) no (1) yes.	0.41
Geneva Towers	Lived in Geneva Towers, San Francisco: (0) no (1) yes. Creston Place, Kansas City, was the reference category.	0.25
Happy about leaving		
Happy about leaving vouchered-out complex	(0) no (1) yes	0.48
Utilization of relocation counseling		
Not aware of counseling services	Index created by crosstabulating awareness of counseling and use of relocation counseling services. Whether not aware of counseling services: (0) no (1) yes.	0.30
Aware of but did not use	Index created by crosstabulating awareness of counseling and use of relocation counseling services. Whether aware of but did not use relocation counseling services: (0) no (1) yes. Used relocation counseling services was the reference category.	0.31
Used services to help in dealings with landlords	Based on results of factor analysis of 13 questions dealing with relocation counseling services. This index measured the number of services utilized to help in dealings with landlords (help in understanding lease agreements, help in dealing with neighborhood and/or landlord problems). Index used for counseled sample regression analysis only ($N = 62$).	0.95
Used services to help with the housing search	Based on results of factor analysis of 13 questions dealing with relocation counseling services. This index measured the number of services utilized to help with the housing search (help listing places, help in choosing neighborhoods to look at). Index used for counseled sample regression analysis only ($N = 62$).	1.22
Used services to help with budgeting	Based on results of factor analysis of 13 questions dealing with relocation counseling services. This index measured the number of services utilized to help with budgeting (help in calculating what the respondent could pay in rent, help in managing the family budget, help in understanding fair housing laws). Index used for counseled sample regression analysis only ($N = 62$).	1.95

Variable	Description	Value
Used services to help complete forms	Based on results of factor analysis of 13 questions dealing with relocation counseling services. This index measured the number of services utilized to help to complete forms (help filling out rental applications, help in filling out applications for HUD, help in setting up utility accounts, help in getting transportation to possible rentals, help in dealing with family problems, help in paying for moving expenses). Index used for counseled sample regression analysis only ($N = 62$).	2.72

Housing search characteristics

Variable	Description	Value
Weeks spent looking	The number of weeks before the respondent moved out of the distressed development that she started to look for a new place to live: (1) under 4, (2) 4 to 7, (3) 8 to 12, (4) more than 12.	2.73
Months spent looking	Months the respondent spent looking for the home moved into directly after leaving distressed development: (1) under 1, (2) 1 to under 2, (3) 2 to under 3, (4) 3 or more.	2.50
Number of places visited	Number of places respondent visited before choosing one to rent: (1) 2 or less, (2) 3 to 5, (3) 6 to 9, (4) 10 or more.	2.49
Considered nearby locations only	Considered only same neighborhood as development or nearby neighborhoods: (0) no (1) yes.	0.21
Considered distant locations only	Considered only other parts of the same city or locations outside the city: (0) no (1) yes.	0.33
Friends/relatives provided information	Found out about current home from friends or relatives: (0) no (1) yes.	0.30
Agencies provided information	Staff person at relocation counseling or housing agency provided information about current home: (0) no (1) yes.	0.21
Distance moved	Miles moved from distressed development to current location. Results ranged from 0.064 to 12.340 miles.	2.15

Neighborhood assessments and indicators

Variable	Description	Value
Very safe near home	Feel very safe near home: (0) no (1) yes.	0.48
Median household income	Median household income in surrounding census tract block. Results ranged from $5,077 to $45,000.	$20,127
Median house value	Median house value in surrounding census tract block. Results ranged from $0 to $422,200.	$78,264
Percent black	Percentage of blacks in surrounding census tract block. Results ranged from 0 to 100 percent.	70.96
Percent owner-occupied	Percentage of houses in surrounding census tract block that are owner occupied. Results ranged from 0 to 100 percent.	35.01

Satisfaction with the housing search

Variable	Description	Value
Very satisfied with housing search	Very satisfied with housing search: (0) no (1) yes.	0.48

Housing satisfaction

Variable	Description	Value
Satisfaction with home	Very satisfied with current house or apartment: (0) no (1) yes.	0.53

TABLE 2.3

Factors Affecting Housing Satisfaction, and Intermediary Variables: Standardized Regression Coefficients
(Total sample)

	Very Satisfied with Home	Very Safe Near Home	Very Satisfied with the Housing Search	Happy about Moving	Not Aware of Counseling
Age	[a]	[a]	[a]	-0.304	[a]
Children	[a]	[a]	[a]	[a]	[a]
Married	-0.191 [a]	[a]	[a]	[a]	[a]
Divorced	[a]	[a]	[a]	0.194	-0.153 [a]
Separated	[a]	[a]	[a]	[a]	[a]
Never married	[a]	[a]	[a]	[a]	[a]
Income	[a]	[a]	[a]	[a]	[a]
Education	[a]	[a]	[a]	[a]	[a]
Employed now	[a]	[a]	[b]	[b]	[b]
Not looking for work now	[a]	[a]	[b]	[b]	[b]
Unemployed now	-0.216	[a]	[b]	[b]	[b]
Welfare	0.189	[a]	[b]	[b]	[b]
Employed at original location	[a]	[a]	[a]	[a]	[a]
Not looking for work at original location	[a]	[a]	[a]	[a]	[a]
Unemployed at original location	[a]	[a]	[a]	[a]	[a]
Length of residence at original location	[a]	[a]	[a]	[a]	[a]
Happy about leaving	[a]	[a]	0.319	[b]	[b]
Crowding, current location	[a]	[a]	[b]	[b]	[b]
Rental burden, current location	0.153	-0.203	[b]	[b]	[b]
Live in a house	0.170 [a]	[a]	[b]	[b]	[b]
Crowding, original location	[a]	[a]	[a]	[a]	[a]

	(1)	(2)	(3)	(4)
Eutaw Gardens	-0.223	a	a	a
Woodsong	a	a	a	-0.243
Geneva Towers	a	a	a	a
Weeks spent looking before moved out	a	b	a	a
Months spent looking	b	b	a	a
Number of places visited	b	b	a	a
Considered nearby locations only	b	b	a	a
Considered distant locations only	b	b	a	a
Agencies provided information	b	b	a	a
Friends/relatives provided information	a	a	a	a
Aware of but did not use counseling services	a	a	a	a
Not aware of counseling services	b	a	-0.163	a
Median household income	b	b	b	a
Median housing prices	b	b	b	0.168
Percentage African American	b	b	b	a
Percentage owner-occuped units	b	b	b	a
Distance moved	b	b	a	a
Very satisfied with housing search	b	b	b	0.219
Very safe near home	b	b	b	0.315
Constant	0.388	2.847	-0.072	0.260
F	9.171	10.245	12.695	10.378
df	2/172	2/172	2/172	8/168
Significance	0.001	0.000	0.000	0.000
Adjusted R Square	0.063	0.096	0.119	0.301

a Variables not meeting tolerance criteria and excluded from regression equation. b Variables not included in regression for logical reasons.

TABLE 2.4

Factors Affecting Housing Satisfaction, and Intermediary Variables: Standardized Regression Coefficients (Counseled sample)

	Very Satisfied with Home	Very Safe Near Home	Very Satisfied with the Housing Search	Number of Places Considered	Considered Close Locations Only
Age	a	a	a	a	0.344
Children	a	a	a	a	a
Married	a	a	0.261	a	a
Divorced	a	a	0.402	a	a
Separated	a	a	a	a	a
Never married	a	a	a	a	a
Income	0.270	a	a	a	a
Education	a	a	a	a	b
Employed now	a	a	b	b	b
Not looking for work now	0.373	a	b	b	b
Unemployed now	a	a	b	b	b
Welfare	a	a	b	b	b
Employed at original location	a	a	a	a	a
Not looking for work at original location	a	a	a	a	a
Unemployed at original location	a	a	a	a	a
Length of residence at original location	a	a	a	a	a
Happy about leaving	a	a	a	a	a
Crowding, current location	a	a	b	b	b
Rental burden, current location	a	-0.325	b	b	b
Live in a house	a	-0.245	b	b	b
Crowding, original location	a	a	a	0.296	a
Eutaw Gardens	a	a	a	a	a

	(1)	(2)	(3)	(4)	(5)
Woodsong	-0.243	a	a	a	a
Geneva Towers	a	a	a	a	a
Weeks spent looking before moved out	a	a	a	a	a
Months spent looking	a	a	a	a	a
Number of places visited	0.214	a	-0.216	a	a
Considered nearby locations only	a	-0.323	a	a	a
Considered distant locations only	a	a	a	a	a
Agencies provided information	a	a	a	a	a
Friends/relatives provided information	a	a	a	a	a
Used services to help in dealings with landlords	a	a	0.307	a	a
Used services to help with the housing search	a	a	a	a	a
Used services to help with budgeting	a	a	a	a	a
Used services to complete forms	a	a	a	a	b
Median household income	0.324	0.324	b	b	b
Median housing prices	-0.364	a	b	b	b
Percentage African American	a	a	b	b	b
Percentage owner-occuped units	a	a	b	b	b
Distance moved	a	a	b	b	b
Very satisfied with housing search	0.224	b	b	b	b
Very safe near home	0.434	b	b	b	b
Constant	0.168	0.393	0.298	1.892	-0.221
F	13.112	6.388	7.835	5.770	8.073
df	8/53	4/57	4/57	1/60	1/60
Significance	0.000	0.000	0.000	0.019	0.006
Adjusted R Square	0.614	0.261	0.309	0.073	0.104

a Variables not meeting tolerance criteria and excluded from regression equation.
b Variables not included in regression for logical reasons.
No factors met tolerance limits for the equation "Used services to help in dealings with landlords."

TABLE 2.5

Indirect, Direct, and Total Effects, Total Sample (*N* = 175)

Variable	Indirect Effect(s)	Direct Effect	Total Effect
Age	−0.021[c]	—	−0.021
Married	—	0.191	0.191
Divorced	0.014[c], 0.015[d]	—	0.019
Unemployed	—	−0.216	−0.216
Welfare	—	0.189	0.189
House	—	0.170	0.170
Rental cost burden	—	0.153	0.153
Median house value	0.053[a]	—	0.053
Woodsong	—	−0.243	−0.243
Eutaw Gardens	0.008[d]	—	0.008
Happy to leave	0.070[b]	—	0.070
Not aware of counseling	−0.036[b]	—	−0.036
Very satisfied with housing search	—	0.219	0.219
Feel very safe	—	0.315	0.315

Note: Indirect through: [a] feel very safe, [b] very satisfied with housing search, [c] happy to leave, [d] not aware of counseling.

multifamily developments that had originally been built by private developers as rental housing. Some had taken advantage of the below-market interest rate financing available under the Section 221(d)(3) program as part of urban renewal projects or targeted toward lower-income tenants. Although privately financed, the Federal Housing Administration (FHA) insured the mortgages. The properties, however, had run into occupancy problems. Some never attracted their intended market; others were not modernized and could not compete with newer developments; still others were mismanaged, not maintained, or located in declining neighborhoods. They had begun to deteriorate and lose residents. Responsible tenants were difficult to attract, and crime escalated.

Foreclosures were not uncommon, and many properties added Section 8 loan management set-asides (LMSAs) during the 1980s to stay afloat. To get an LMSA, an owner had to demonstrate that if the property did not receive subsidized rents, it would not be able to maintain an occupancy level sufficient to make its mortgage payments; the LMSA was needed to prevent a default on the mortgage and a claim against the FHA insurance fund. The LMSAs guaranteed that HUD would expend a certain amount of budget authority for a set number of units at the development. Because an owner could receive multiple LMSAs, HUD might be

TABLE 2.6

Indirect, Direct, and Total Effects, Counseled Sample (*N* = 62)

Variable	Indirect Effect(s)	Direct Effect	Total Effect
Age	0.074[c]	—	0.074
Married	0.058[b]	—	0.058
Divorced	0.090[b]	—	0.090
Income	—	0.270	0.270
Not looking for work	—	0.373	0.373
Rental burden	−0.141[a]	—	−0.141
House	−0.106[a]	—	−0.106
Crowding, original location	−0.014[d]	—	−0.014[d]
Woodsong	—	−0.243	−0.243
Median housing prices	—	−0.364	−0.364
Median household income	0.141[a]	—	0.141[a]
Number of places considered	−0.048[b]	—	−0.048
Considered close locations only	−0.137[a]	—	−0.137
Used services to help deal with landlords	0.069[b]	—	0.069
Very satisfied with housing search	—	0.224	0.224
Feel very safe	—	0.434	0.434

Note: Indirect through: [a] feel very satisfied; [b] very satisfied with housing search; [c] considered close neighborhoods only; [d] number of places considered.

subsidizing large numbers of units at one property. These units were filled by Section 8 tenants who began to move into the properties. HUD further assisted properties by granting owners flexible subsidy funds to use for capital improvements or for deferred maintenance items. The flexible subsidy funds were payable at the end of the mortgage or in the event of a default.

These curative actions, however, were, in the words of one HUD official, a "Band-Aid at best" (Schrader 1996). Conditions at some of the properties became so deplorable that by the mid-1990s, HUD had determined that the best course of action—and the most cost-effective—was to close down the most troubled properties. Reflecting the shift in HUD policy from project-based assistance to tenant-based assistance occurring at that time, the residents were given vouchers that they could use in housing units of their own choice in the private market. Vouchering out the properties took place under the direction of HUD headquarters in Washington with the involvement of the HUD field office, the local housing authority, the on-site management company, and often, companies providing counseling services.

The Four Study Properties

Four severely distressed and mismanaged developments were chosen for
the study: Eutaw Gardens in Baltimore; Woodsong Apartments in Newport News, Virginia; Creston Place in Kansas City, Missouri; and Geneva
Towers in San Francisco. The selection of these four properties was based
on several criteria, including geographic diversity, the tightness or open-
ness of the local housing market, the number of tenants, and the presence
of conditions unique to a site.[9]

The properties ranged in size from Creston Place in Kansas City,
with 72 units, to Geneva Towers in San Francisco, with 576 units. At the
time they were vouchered out, the four developments contained a total of
798 households. The following numbers of residents at each site were interviewed in the telephone survey: Baltimore, 54; Newport News, 83; Kansas City, 13; and San Francisco, 51. Most of the respondents were black
female single parents.[10] The average age was 41 years. Income levels were
low, with 46 percent reporting incomes of less than $5,000; 37 percent
had not completed high school; and only 35 percent reported working either full or part time. Forty-one percent were recipients of Aid to Families with Dependent Children. Table 2.7 presents the demographic
characteristics of the residents surveyed at each site and summarizes the
background characteristics of the four properties.

Eutaw Gardens, Baltimore

Eutaw Gardens, located in Baltimore's Bolton Hill neighborhood, was built
in 1972 by a nonprofit organization under the Section 221(d)(3) Below
Market Interest Rate program. The development bordered Madison Park,
a moderate-income black area with historic brownstone townhouses; and
the North Avenue section of Reservoir Hill, a lower-income black area
with significant housing abandonment.[11] The development contained 268
units in 18 four-story buildings. The configuration and the development's
red brick buildings set it apart from the adjacent gentrified neighborhoods,
as did its residents—predominantly black nonworking single mothers.[12]

The property experienced management and financial problems almost from the beginning. In 1976, the property was transferred to a new
owner, and the development received 134 units of Section 8 LMSA subsidies. The property was awarded $902,693 in assistance in 1980 and an

TABLE 2.7

Background Characteristics Compared

Characteristic	Eutaw Gardens	Woodsong	Creston Place	Geneva Towers
Local housing market	Soft, with large supply of affordable rental units; 9% rental vacancy rate; ample supply of units below FMR levels	Soft, with large supply of affordable rental units; 1995 estimated rental vacancy rate, 7.5%; ample supply of units below FMR levels	Soft overall, extremely soft rental market; among lowest housing costs in country; 1990 city rental vacancy rate, 12%; ample supply of units below FMR levels	Tight, low vacancy rates; among highest housing costs in country; rental market loosened slightly in 1994
Political and bureaucratic environment	Housing scandals at HABC; vouchering programs highly controversial due to reclustering in "fragile" neighborhoods	High-profile property; SWAT involvement; NNRHA, a well-run agency, administered large assisted housing program	HAKC, a troubled agency, under court receivership; MHDC in KC also administered Section 8 vouchers and certificates	HUD foreclosed on property in 1991; HUD takeover of SFHA in 1996 (after vouchering out of Geneva Towers)
Type of neighborhood	Located at boundary of 3 neighborhoods: Bolton Hill (a gentrified neighborhood); Madison Park (moderate-income, black, brownstone townhouses); and North Avenue section of Reservoir Hill (lower-income, black, significant housing abandonment)	Modest residential neighborhood; apartment complexes and single-family homes; 2 miles from old CBD	Urban neighborhood; mix of residential, commercial, institutional, and industrial uses; once very beautiful residential neighborhood, troubled and deteriorated but signs of gentrification	Residential neighborhood; attached and detached housing units, average to good quality; in one of SF's southernmost neighborhoods
Number of units	268	480	72	576
Type and age of buildings	18 4-story buildings, red brick exteriors; community building included; built 1972	62 2-story buildings, brick veneer and wood siding exteriors, each served by breezeway; built 1970	3 4-story buildings connected by bridges; one elevator served all 3 buildings; built during 1920s	2 high-rise prestressed concrete towers; appeared out of place in neighborhood; no

(continued)

45

TABLE 2.7 (continued)

Characteristic	Eutaw Gardens	Woodsong	Creston Place	Geneva Towers
				playgrounds, not designed for families; built 1964
Total number of voucher recipients	161	321	35	262
Sample number of voucher recipients interviewed on household survey	54	83	13	51
Average number of years lived at site [HS]	9.1	4.1	3.4	11.8
Characteristics of voucher recipients at time of vouchering out [HS]	98% black; 82% not married; 54% with children; 33% working	98% black; 87% not married; 72% with children; 30% working	100% black; 92% not married; 92% with children; 46% working	82% black; 60% not married; 67% with children; 16% working
Vouchering-out dates	September 1995–April 1996	May 1995–February 1996	August 1994–October 1994	March 1995–January 1996

Note: HS refers to information derived from the household survey.

additional $214,966 in 1981. During the 1980s, the complex was managed by at least six different management companies, one of which was notorious for buying up properties of this nature and extracting what it could from them. A 1994 comprehensive management review by the HUD Baltimore office rated the development "unsatisfactory" and concluded that more than $4 million was needed for repairs. Crime was also a serious problem at Eutaw Gardens. Neighbors in Bolton Hill and Madison Park said that burglars and muggers used the complex's interior courtyards to hide from police because they were not visible from the street.

In September 1994, Eutaw Gardens went into default, and in March 1995, the property was assigned to HUD. In April, HUD officially rejected a proposal from a consultant to purchase and rehabilitate the property because of the extent of its deterioration. In June 1995, HUD was designated mortgagee-in-possession (MIP), and the vouchering-out process began. At Eutaw Gardens, the HUD field office, the local housing authority, the management company, and relocation agencies conducted the vouchering-out process (table 2.8 summarizes the vouchering out process at Eutaw Gardens and at the three other vouchering-out sites).

The HUD field office in Baltimore performed a variety of duties, including requesting vouchers, handling administrative duties associated with an MIP property, arranging architectural and engineering reports, working with the local housing authority, supervising the on-site management company, and providing moving allowances and assistance to residents. In addition, the field office played a central role in rumor control by organizing meetings and publishing newsletters to inform residents about the vouchering-out process and the status of the property.

The Housing Authority of Baltimore City (HABC) was responsible for administering the voucher program, determining the eligibility of tenants, inspecting the units selected by the tenants, and issuing the vouchers. ARCO, the private company that managed Eutaw Gardens at the time of the vouchering out, selected and monitored the relocation counseling agencies. In addition, it (1) worked with tenants to prepare them to move, (2) worked with HABC on housing inspections at new locations, (3) worked with landlords (e.g., ARCO provided landlords with credit information so that they could screen tenants), (4) hired a moving company, and (5) handled all the details of the moving process.

Two nonprofit organizations, Communities Organized to Improve Life (COIL) and Saint Pius V Housing Committee, provided relocation

TABLE 2.8

Vouchering-Out Process Compared

Characteristic	Eutaw Gardens	Woodsong	Creston Place	Geneva Towers

Role of HUD Field Office	• Conducted public relations and rumor control
	• Organized two meetings with residents
	• Published newsletter
	• Asset Manager handled tenant inquiries
	• Prepared "Model Relocation Plan," detailing HUD-Baltimore's experiences
	• Eased difficulties when tenants learned that they would have to be recertified to use vouchers in Baltimore County
	• Provided following waivers for HABC:
	  1. Families allowed to look for homes beyond 120-day limit
	  2. Families could rent housing units the same size as current unit
		• Performed administrative work associated with MIP, arranging A&E reports, requesting vouchers, etc.
		• Oversaw vouchering-out process, met with residents and resident council
		• Supervised on-site management company
		• Conducted public relations and rumor control
		• Designated the Asset Manager "focal point" for all parties involved in process
		• Worked out moving allowance payment standard based on unit size and distance moved
			• Performed administrative work associated with MIP, arranging A&E reports, requesting vouchers, etc.
			• Provided moving assistance
				• Performed administrative work associated with MIP, arranging A&E reports, requesting vouchers, etc.
				• Provided moving assistance
				• Developed vouchering-out process jointly with SFHA
				• Participated in training counselors; assisted counselors throughout process
				• Prepared Moving Allowance Relocation Package of Incentives, which included a set amount for moving allowance and reimbursement for utility connection costs
				• In daily contact with SFHA and counselors to help in decision making

Role of local housing authority	HABC: In general, HABC treated vouchering-out tenants as it	NNRHA: • Checked residents' documents to determine eligibility for vouchers	HAKC, under court receivership, had no role; Missouri Housing Development Commission	SFHA taken over by HUD after vouchering out. Prior to takeover:

Name and role of on-site management company				
would any other voucher recipients • Determined eligibility of tenants for vouchers • Issued vouchers • Inspected units and processed leasing agreements ARCO, Inc. • Selected and monitored counseling agencies • Worked with tenants to help them move • Worked with HABC on housing inspections • Worked with landlords, providing credit information and security deposits • Hired moving company • Handled details of moving process	• Met with residents to tell them about the voucher program • Gave residents briefing package with information on apartment options, portability, and factors to consider in choosing housing • Processed and issued vouchers • Inspected units • Ran check to see if residents owed HA any money • Went on-site toward end of vouchering-out to meet with residents • Transported some residents to look for housing Intown Properties, Inc. • Determined priority by which residents received vouchers • Secured subcontractor to supply relocation services • Issued moving allowances • Applied moving allowances to debts residents owed NNRHA • Issued security deposit refunds to residents • Issued bus tickets to residents to use in their housing search • Counseled residents on	performed standard administrative tasks including income verification, processing vouchers, inspecting units. It also: • Held individual one-to-one meetings at property • Provided budgeting assistance • Helped residents schedule movers • Helped residents contact social services agencies, if necessary; provided short-term loans to cover utility deposits • Provided listings of private landlords accepting Section 8 Connor Management (property manager at time of HUD takeover): • Erroneously informed residents that property would be closed within two days Jury-Tiehen HD, Inc. (new property manager installed by HUD after takeover): • Instituted strict security provisions, including metal detectors at doors and armed guards	• Negotiated MOU with HUD for complex to be demolished and city to build new units • Developed vouchering-out process jointly with HUD • Was in charge of coordinating activities of property manager, counselors, and tenants • Administered voucher program • Encouraged tenants to see program as an opportunity Republic Management • Secured subcontractor to supply relocation services • Provided counseling services after original group proved unsuccessful

(continued)

TABLE 2.8 (continued)

Characteristic	Eutaw Gardens	Woodsong	Creston Place	Geneva Towers
		housekeeping skills as part of regular management function • Helped motivate and encourage residents • Evicted troublesome tenants prior to issuing of vouchers	• Managed property during vouchering out	
Agency providing counseling	COIL and subcontractor, St. Pius V Housing Committee • Nonprofit community housing agencies from West Baltimore	MTB Investments and subcontractor Cassaundra Williams • Private company that provides a variety of housing-related services and professional relocation specialist	Missouri Housing Development Commission • State agency providing financing for multifamily and single-family housing; administers Section 8 certificates and vouchers throughout Kansas City metropolitan area; no special counseling provided for Creston Place residents	Group 1: Merger of independent consultants replaced by: Group 2: Republic Management took over in-house; retained 2 of original counselors and added own staff to form 10-person division; trained counselors and provided them with support services and resources

counseling to Eutaw Gardens families for a fee of $450 per family.[13] Six relocation counselors worked with Eutaw Gardens residents. Families were provided with an information packet that included a list of area landlords, newspaper listings, and an apartment-shopper guidebook to assist in the housing search. Counselors did not, however, take tenants to look at housing units. Table 2.9 compares the relocation counseling models at the four vouchered-out sites with the MTO model (Feins, Holin, and Phipps 1994).

A major advantage of using two Baltimore City community-based agencies for relocation counseling was that it enabled HUD to set up a viable counseling program relatively quickly. In addition, there is little question that the counselors helped move residents into better housing within a short time period. However, there also were a number of problems with the Baltimore counseling. First, the counselors' negative views on suburban locations may have discouraged a wider range of moves.[14] One of the counselors, the director of one of the two community-based housing organizations, in weighing the merits of housing alternatives, emphasized the accessibility of shopping in the city over access to better schools in the suburbs:

> We attempted to ask questions that people wouldn't consider within the intensity of the moment, like: "If you get this wonderful new apartment— you have lived across from this full-service grocery store for 20 years now, and you move to a location where the nearest grocery store is two miles away. How are you going to go there and get back with a full bag of groceries?" These were things that people hadn't thought about, especially those who had entertained the notion of moving to the suburban areas, the great green pastures. (COIL housing counselor)

Second, despite the importance that landlord informants in Baltimore attached to poor housekeeping practices among Section 8 tenants, virtually no attention was devoted to the subject during counseling sessions. Third, Eutaw Gardens relocation counselors lacked adequate training. In both agencies, the counselors' experience was with helping current and prospective homeowners, not with relocating renters. Fourth, record keeping was somewhat casual; this limited the ability to use the records to monitor what happened to clients. Fifth, counselors lacked a uniform counseling strategy. Because the HUD Baltimore office did not provide much direction for the content of the counseling, the counselors did what they knew best. One of the counselors emphasized the importance of better budgeting. A second counselor, conversely, thought that her clients already

TABLE 2.9

Relocation Counseling Characteristics Compared

Characteristic	Eutaw Gardens	Woodsong	Creston Place	Geneva Towers
Agency providing counseling	COIL and subcontractor, St. Pius V Housing Committee • Nonprofit community housing agencies from West Baltimore	MTB Investments and subcontractor Cassaundra Williams • Private company that provides a variety of housing-related services and professional relocation specialist	Missouri Housing Development Commission • State agency providing financing for multifamily and single-family housing, administers Section 8 certificates and vouchers throughout Kansas City metropolitan area; no special counseling provided for Creston Place residents	Republic Management • Secured subcontractor to supply relocation services • Provided counseling services after original group proved unsuccessful
Counseling agency strengths	• Knew city • Was able to set up and implement relocation counseling operation quickly	• Followed procedures used successfully in other relocations • Home office support freed counselor to concentrate on residents' needs • Relocation counselor was positive role model for residents • As outsider, no preconceived notions of where residents "ought" to live or where they might be "welcome" • MTB was paid when resident relocated; timing of payment helped speed up process	• Fast and efficient • Experienced in administering Section 8 program • Knew city • Knew landlords willing to take Section 8 tenants	Group 1: • Some individual counselors knew resident population and were experienced in social service assistance programs Group 2: • Hired best and most experienced counselors from Group 1 • Offering counseling in-house provided Geneva Towers residents with one-stop set of services, from help finding housing to counseling about personal problems
Counseling agency weaknesses	• Not experienced in helping renters relocate to new neighborhoods	• Only one counselor, and success of counseling largely dependent on the personality and skill of	• Lacked time to perform more and better counseling services	Group 1: • Individuals had different approaches

• Devoted inadequate attention to behavioral issues like good housekeeping • Counselors lacked uniform counseling strategy	that individual • Needed to learn city		• Individuals had no experience working together Group 2: • None identified
Cost of counseling services $450 per family	$348 per family	Regular administrative fee given under the Section 8 program	$500 per family
Number of Counselors 6	1	4, none full time	10
Counseling Services Provided • Counseled families through relocation process • Provided help where needed (dealt with school transfers; helped obtain records from Social Security Administration) • Helped with budgeting • Provided detailed information about areas preferred by clients Other attributes of the counseling • Counseling not mandatory • Office open evenings and during weekends • No counseling on housekeeping • Extensive help required by "holdouts," last 7 families remaining at Eutaw Gardens	• One-to-one counseling • Credit and budgeting help • Negotiated lower security deposits and waiver of credit check fees • Made referrals to community resources; arranged for volunteer counselors • Looked for landlords who would accept Section 8 clients; educated them on the program • Located affordable housing and larger units, published listings of available units, brought landlords to the site • Preinspected units to make sure they met Section 8 Housing Quality Standards • Held workshops and monthly "Town Hall"-type meetings on search techniques, negotiating with landlords, and dealing with stress of moving • Accompanied residents with special needs to look for housing	• No special counseling called for in contract; instead, called for relocation in shortest time frame possible • One-to-one meetings held with each tenant by an MHDC staff member • Provided information on Section 8 rules • Helped tenants schedule moving vans • Provided budgeting assistance • Provided help in contacting social service agencies for assistance in resolving specific problems Other attributes of the counseling: • Residents had already gone through income verification procedure; no need to check	Group 1: • Information not available Group 2: • Held landlord presentation event • Advertised in newspaper • Provided one-to-one assistance to find housing • Traveled with tenants to potential new units • Provided counseling about personal problems • Negotiated with SFHA on allowable search expenses

practiced good budgeting. She, unlike some of the other counselors, pro-
moted suburban moves so that clients could take advantage of suburban
job opportunities and live in neighborhoods where self-sufficiency was the
norm.

Nevertheless, the vouchering out at Eutaw Gardens went smoothly
during a period when housing vouchers were highly controversial in Baltimore.[15] Vouchering out began in September 1995, and by March 1996,
all 161 households had relocated. Strategic planning at the outset—meeting with local politicians early in the process—helped the HUD Baltimore staff avoid major mistakes. Using two community-based housing
agencies for the relocation counseling also may have sped up the relocation process, but, as indicated above, had drawbacks as well.

Woodsong, Newport News, Virginia

Woodsong was located in Newport News, Virginia, which is a long, nar-
row city situated on a peninsula northeast of Hampton Roads, one of the
great natural harbors of the world. The neighboring city of Hampton occu-
pies the lower part of the peninsula east of Newport News.[16] Containing
69 square miles and stretching 20 miles in length, Newport News is one
of the larger cities in the state in land area. Its consolidation in 1958 combined the older downtown central city with largely undeveloped land to
the northwest. During the mid-1980s, a building boom in this area drained
the southern end of the city, known as the "East End," of much of its commercial activity, leaving behind a concentration of low-income minority
residents. Woodsong was located two miles north of Newport News's old
central business district and on the northern edge of the East End.

Woodsong was originally built as market housing targeted to shipyard workers. It was a low-rise, sprawling 480-unit development covering
26 acres. Constructed in 1968 and 1970 in two phases, the development
consisted of 62 two-story buildings with brick veneer and wood-siding
exteriors. The surrounding neighborhood was predominantly residential,
with apartment developments and modest single-family homes.

For Woodsong's financing, the owner took advantage of the Section
221(d)(3) Below Market Interest Rate program. Following the sale of the
property to a new owner in 1980, Woodsong began experiencing occupancy problems. In the early 1980s, a flexible subsidy for substantial rehabilitation was granted; Section 8 LMSA subsidies were added

throughout the decade. Moderate-income households, however, moved farther north in the city, where new development was occurring.

By the early 1990s, Woodsong had become notorious for drug activity, gunfire, and fighting. Physical conditions deteriorated to such an extent that a physical inspection in the mid-1990s showed that 465 of the 480 units could not meet HUD's Housing Quality Standards. Woodsong topped HUD's 1994 list of the 25 most troubled subsidized housing developments in the country and was used to illustrate the deplorable conditions of properties allowed to decay while their landlords profited from government subsidies.[17] When HUD headquarters made requests in September 1994 for distressed properties that might be candidates for review by the Special Workout Assistance Team (SWAT), Woodsong was one of five properties nominated by the Richmond Field Office.[18]

SWAT's involvement, political pressure, and the national prominence of the owner (Insignia Financial Group) as a provider of real estate services made any action taken at Woodsong a high-profile matter. When HUD refused to bail out Insignia in February 1995, Insignia agreed to turn over the property to HUD under a voluntary MIP agreement; HUD took over as MIP in March 1995. However, it was not until September— six months later, and four and a half months after the relocation specialist had arrived on site—that HUD confirmed with the residents that Woodsong would be closed permanently and all the residents relocated.

After taking over as MIP, HUD brought in Intown Properties to manage Woodsong. Intown managed the property during the vouchering-out phase, updated tenant records, issued payments for moving expenses and security deposits, and secured a subcontractor to provide relocation counseling services. The Newport News Redevelopment and Housing Authority certified the residents' eligibility for the vouchers, issued vouchers, and inspected units. Toward the end of the process, the authority met with residents on-site and provided transportation for residents to look for housing. (Table 2.8 summarizes the vouchering-out process.)

MTB, a private company specializing in housing-related services, was hired to provide the counseling services for Woodsong residents (see table 2.9). MTB subcontracted with an independent relocation specialist to do the on-site counseling. The final cost for counseling averaged $348 per family. The counseling services provided for Woodsong's residents were the most extensive of the four sites. MTB's approach was thorough and focused: Fourteen separate activities were included in the relocation services contract.[19]

To assist residents in the housing search, MTB and its relocation specialist did not rely solely on housing authority lists, as some counseling agencies at the other sites did, but instead attempted to expand housing choice by bringing new landlords into the Section 8 program. The relocation specialist visited "mom and pop" real estate agencies (agencies not associated with a franchise company) to find housing for the residents. These agencies represented owners of single-family structures located in areas of interest to some Woodsong residents, particularly the East End of Newport News. The relocation specialist called property managers of other developments, and she set up a booth at an annual apartment conference held in Newport News so that she could hand out business cards, make contacts, and find referrals for the residents. These efforts resulted in an estimated 36 new landlords coming into the Section 8 program—20 in Newport News and 16 in nearby Hampton.[20]

The relocation specialist gave residents the lists of the complexes she had found with the addresses and names of the contacts. The residents were expected to choose among the options and to follow up with the landlords on their own, but the relocation specialist provided special assistance to those who needed it. Beyond the basic relocation services, MTB attempted to inspire residents to try to improve their lot in life, pointing out the new opportunities that a housing voucher afforded them. The relocation specialist held monthly meetings—she called them "town hall" meetings—with the Woodsong tenants. In addition to providing information about the relocation process, these town hall meetings were used to motivate the residents and hone their house-hunting skills.

This approach—providing counseling through a private company with expertise in such services—appeared to work well in the Newport News case, at least in terms of a smooth vouchering-out process.[21] The company, which was paid as each family was relocated, had an incentive to proceed as expeditiously as possible; this incentive moved the process along. Further, as an outside agency, it had no preconceived notion of where tenants "ought" to live, nor did it rely solely on the housing authority's lists of developments accepting Section 8 tenants. As a result, the housing search was not limited to known areas of the city or to known landlords. The success of this approach, however, is largely dependent on the person hired to do the on-site counseling. In the case of Newport News, that person's personality, energy, drive, resourcefulness, and tact were, according to informants, key to her effectiveness.

The Woodsong relocation started slowly while the paperwork authorizing the closing of the development was being processed and the administrative procedures were being worked out. Once under way, however, relocation proceeded quickly; 321 vouchers were issued, with more than 300 processed between June and December 1995. The professionalism and dedication of the staffs, the cooperation among key actors, and the hiring of experienced professionals to provide the counseling contributed to the efficiency of the vouchering-out process at Woodsong.

Creston Place, Kansas City, Missouri

Creston Place was in Kansas City, which in most respects is a typical older industrial city in the Midwest. The metropolitan area, however, is split almost in half by the state line along the Missouri River between Missouri and Kansas. This line has been a relatively impenetrable barrier for low-income households and minorities as more prosperous families and businesses have moved out of Kansas City (and to a lesser extent out of the adjoining Kansas City, Kansas) to the area southwest of the city.

Creston Place was located in the urban neighborhood of Hyde Park, which lies on the border between Kansas City's downtown and midtown areas. Once a beautiful residential neighborhood, at the time of the vouchering out, Hyde Park contained a mix of troubled and deteriorated residential, commercial, and industrial uses. Gentrification of some fine older homes had begun, however.

Creston Place was the oldest and smallest of the four case study properties. Built in the 1920s, it contained 72 units in three four-story buildings that were connected by bridges.[22] Other buildings of almost identical design and location remained in the neighborhood and continued to operate as private unassisted housing, but over the years, Creston Place had been allowed to deteriorate. The buildings were rehabilitated using Section 236 assistance in 1974. The development also received Section 8 LMSA assistance in an effort to keep it viable when it subsequently experienced financial trouble. The buildings, however, deteriorated further. The units were infested with rats and insects, making them generally unfit for use, and eventually, a criminal element moved in. In the last six months of 1993, 14 assaults and 2 suicides were reported at Creston Place; in early 1994, a visitor was shot.

By 1994, political pressure was mounting to do something about

Creston Place. HUD needed to obtain control of the property before it could take any significant steps to resolve the development's problems. HUD asked the mortgagee—the Federal National Mortgage Association (formerly nicknamed and now officially named Fannie Mae)—to take possession of Creston Place and to appoint a receiver. In May 1994, Fannie Mae took possession of the property and assigned it to HUD.

Because the local housing authority was under court receivership, the Missouri Housing Development Commission (MHDC) administered the Creston Place vouchering out. MHDC determined the eligibility of tenants, inspected the units selected by the tenants, and issued the vouchers. The focus of the Creston Place vouchering-out effort was the immediate demolition of the crime-infested buildings; counseling tenants was not given a high priority. MHDC agreed to be compensated by the standard administrative fee given under the Section 8 program.

MHDC's staff, moving very quickly to assist Creston Place's tenants, conducted a series of meetings at the property. These were one-to-one meetings between each tenant household and an MHDC staff member; no group meetings were held. The staff of MHDC believed that close, individual contact between the housing case managers and the tenants would better serve the tenants' needs. The small number of tenants qualifying for vouchers also helped make this approach feasible; initially, 35 Creston Place families received vouchers.[23] In addition, the tenants were already receiving Section 8 assistance through the LMSA program and were therefore aware of the income certification process required to qualify for the vouchers.

Meetings were held over a two- to three-day period and were conducted by two to four staff members each day. Each tenant was informed of the benefits that he or she would receive, provided with household budgeting guidance, and assisted in scheduling a move. When necessary, tenants were put in touch with social service agencies that could help them with specific problems. Such assistance included the provision of short-term loans to pay for utility deposits until reimbursement was received from HUD.

Because of the small size of the development and the desire to find a quick solution to crime problems in the building, the relocation model followed in the Kansas City case study was not elaborate. No special provisions were made for counseling the Creston Place tenants, nor did tenants receive assistance beyond that given to any other recipient of a Section 8 voucher. Each tenant was provided with HUD and MHDC lists of developments that accepted Section 8 vouchers. Tenants were expected to find rental units using these lists, the newspapers, or their own contacts. Although the tenants were moved quickly and efficiently, there were a number of limitations to this model. First, the housing search was limited to areas of the city known by the tenants. Second, no special services were offered to instruct tenants in search techniques or to help them cope with the stress of moving. (See tables 2.8 and 2.9 for summaries of the vouchering-out process and the counseling.)

Creston Place's tenants were relocated into alternative housing within 60 days of receiving notification that the development would be closed. The small size of the development contributed to the speed with which relocation took place. The skill and perseverance of MHDC staff also added to the efficiency, as did expediting the inspection and approval of the voucher recipients' new units.

Geneva Towers, San Francisco

Geneva Towers was located in San Francisco. Long considered the financial hub of the Bay Area, San Francisco is one of three major urban centers within this densely populated region. The region's largest city, San Jose, lies approximately 55 miles to the south. The city of Oakland is located directly east of San Francisco across the bay. Demand for housing in San Francisco has been exceptionally strong, resulting in very low vacancy rates, together with some of the highest housing costs in the country. At the time the tenants of Geneva Towers started their search for housing (in 1994), however, the market had softened slightly due to an economic recession.

Geneva Towers was located in Visitacion Valley, one of San Francisco's southernmost communities. With 576 units, Geneva Towers was the largest of the four developments selected for the vouchered-out study. Built in 1964, it consisted of two high-rise towers constructed of pre-stressed concrete. The development was originally meant to house middle-income workers employed at San Francisco International Airport; it was not designed to accommodate families with children. A quiet residential neighborhood, Visitacion Valley contained predominantly small, single-family detached and attached housing units. It had a high rate of homeownership, a relatively high median income and median house value, and a lower rate of crime than the city as a whole—characteristics that made the high-rise Geneva Towers structure and its residents an unwelcome presence in the community.

Two years after construction, the private owners refinanced Geneva Towers with HUD mortgage insurance in order to qualify as low-income housing. Ten years later (in 1976), HUD granted the property Section 8 assistance. Geneva Towers primarily attracted families as tenants, even though it lacked multiple-bedroom units and outdoor play areas. This mismatch between the property's intended and actual uses created management problems. Significant deterioration occurred, and the absence of internal security allowed crime to escalate.

In 1991, HUD foreclosed on the property and hired a local affordable housing management and development company to manage and improve it. Although the company succeeded in lowering the crime rate, a structural review showed that all the physical systems required major renovation. In 1992, HUD concluded that rehabilitation of the property for family housing was not feasible. It also decided that although rehabilitation for senior housing might be possible, it was not appropriate for this location. Therefore, HUD decided to close and demolish the entire facility as soon as the residents could be relocated.

Three main agencies participated in the vouchering out of Geneva Towers: the HUD San Francisco field office, the San Francisco Housing Authority (SFHA), and the San Francisco Mayor's Office of Housing (MOH). (See table 2.8 for a summary of the vouchering-out process.) HUD and SFHA developed the process jointly. MOH monitored the progress of the vouchering-out process, but it did not have a direct role in the counseling program or in the vouchering-out process. It also was involved in the development of a memorandum of understanding reached by the city, HUD, the SFHA, and the community regarding the closure of Geneva Towers and the subsequent redevelopment of the property.

The role of the San Francisco HUD field office in the vouchering-out process was unique among the four case studies in that it played a key role in training and supervising counselors. The Geneva Towers vouchering out demonstrates yet another model in providing counseling services. In this case, the on-site property management firm, Republic Management, initially hired several independent consultants and merged them into a group to provide the necessary services.[24] After several months, this merger had proved unsuccessful; the consultants, who had no experience working together, had different approaches. As a result, Republic took on the counseling function in-house. The firm retained two of the original counselors and reorganized some of its own staff into a ten-person relocation division that provided a one-stop set of services, ranging from assistance in identifying housing alternatives to counseling about personal problems. The fee received by Republic was $500 for each household placed successfully in new housing. The counselors were given a basic training course and were provided with a variety of support services and resources; they were also given a great deal of flexibility in the methods they could use to accomplish their relocation task.

Tenants were asked to set up individual appointments with a housing counselor to discuss their housing needs and desires. With the residents' permission, the counselors ran credit checks to avoid problems that might surface when the new landlords inquired into the tenants' credit history. After the initial appointment, the counselors met weekly with the tenants.

To assist in the search for new housing, Republic prepared a list of housing possibilities assembled from various sources, including area newspapers, housing authority lists, and direct referrals. Republic counselors also advertised for apartment leads in local newspapers and organization newsletters, drafted letters to property managers of residential buildings in the neighborhood to inquire about openings, and regularly drove through neighborhoods looking for "for rent" signs. Leads on available units were then matched with residents' requirements and wishes. In most cases, the new landlord was contacted initially by a counselor to ascertain unit availability, timing, and requirements. The designated resident was then sent to meet the landlord and to look at the unit. If requested, a housing counselor would accompany the tenant. Tenants also received cab fare to travel to units under consideration.

Once desirable units were found, counselors assisted in negotiating and completing the transactions with the landlords, setting up utility accounts, arranging for movers, packing, preparing certification paperwork to obtain the housing vouchers from the San Francisco Housing Authority, guiding residents through the certification process, and coordinating housing unit inspections by the housing authority.

The Geneva Towers model resembled that of Woodsong in the number and variety of services provided, but it differed in that the services were provided by multiple counselors hired and supervised by the on-site management firm. Further, unlike the Woodsong counselor, the counselors at Geneva Towers did not follow a set plan of action. (Table 2.9 compares

TABLE 2.10

Destination Neighborhoods Compared

Characteristic	Eutaw Gardens	Woodsong	Creston Place	Geneva Towers
Geographical aspects of the move				
• Mean distance	• 1.98 miles	• 2.83 miles	• 3.42 miles	• 4.13 miles
• Proportion moving 5.1 miles or more	• 7%	• 20%, mostly to the northern part of Newport News	• 10%	• 24%
• Proportion remaining in the neighborhood of origin	• 40% remained in West Baltimore	• 18% remained in the Briarfield section of Newport News	• One-third remained in the immediate area, moving less than 2 miles away	• 9% remained in Visitacion Valley
• Proportion remaining in city of origin	• 90%; additional 10% moved to Baltimore County	• 76%; 22% moved to neighboring city of Hampton	• 100%	• 80%; 18% moved to other cities in Bay Area including 5% to Oakland
Destination neighborhoods	West Baltimore (location of Eutaw Gardens) • Includes diverse neighborhoods (public housing, gentrified, black low-income rental) • Housing abandonment and deterioration are side-by-side with architecturally significant buildings	Briarfield (location of Woodsong) • A large group moved across the street to an older but attractive rental complex with townhouse units and winding streets	Downtown (location of Creston Place) • Many tenants stayed in the Hyde Park neighborhood in the Downtown area • Many businesses are closing and migrating to the suburbs • Area suffers from a serious crime problem	Visitacion Valley (location of Geneva Towers) • One of San Francisco's southernmost communities • Contains mostly single-family attached and detached homes • Area has a lower crime rate than the city as a whole

- Depending on the destination block, a move within West Baltimore may or may not represent an improvement in quality of life

Cherry Hill
- Predominantly black, low-income rental community in South Baltimore
- Community contains a high proportion of low-rise public housing currently undergoing modernization

Dickeyville-Franklintown
- A combination of higher-status homeownership neighborhoods with middle-status, predominantly black communities on western edge of city
- Clearly, a more suburban-type environment with more greenery than in West Baltimore, but schools are not better
- Crime is less of a problem than in West Baltimore, but schools are not better

Newsome Park
- Contains a small neighborhood of single-family homes dating back to World War I
- Most moved to a well-maintained and well-managed townhouse apartment development

Southeast Community
- An older area containing mostly single-family homes, some of which have been converted to multiple units
- Pockets of deteriorated housing and marginal apartment complexes
- Some relocatees may be worse off than at Woodsong

North Newport News
- Considered a better area than Woodsong (newer, higher income, and fewer families rely on public assistance)
- Some signs of distress in development to which most Woodsong families moved (trash nearby and graffiti)

Bayview/Hunters Point
- Geographically isolated section of the city; area is best known for location of Hunters Point shipyard
- Area has a mix of underutilized industrial uses and older housing units
- Socioeconomic level is lower than Visitacion Valley
- Multifamily building conditions are poor
- Relocatees experienced a lower quality of life

Midtown/South
- Tenants relocated to 3-story apartments of pre–World War II vintage
- Area has a great deal of deterioration, to an extent associated with presence of adult entertainment businesses

East/Central
- Those who moved into Hilltop Homes (1960s garden apartments) found good housing, a lot of open space, ample parking, and safer conditions
- Larger families who moved into single-family dwellings experienced poor housing conditions

Western Addition
- Part of the central core of San Francisco, a socioeconomically and ethnically diverse area with a dense development pattern
- Significant portions of the area have experienced gentrification
- Contains an active commercial sector and plentiful green space and playgrounds
- In general, this area offers a similar or higher quality of life for Geneva Towers residents

(continued)

TABLE 2.10 (continued)

Characteristic	Eutaw Gardens	Woodsong	Creston Place	Geneva Towers
Destination neighborhoods (continued)	Highland Village • An affordable rental complex in economically depressed southwest Baltimore County • Relocatees experienced little improvement in job opportunities but experienced improvement in school quality Park Heights (Edgecomb and Cylburn) • Relocatees concentrated in garden development built on a hillside; erosion and litter are problems • Neighborhoods have a serious crime problem • Quality of life is not significantly higher than at Eutaw Gardens	Denbigh • A newer, suburban-type area in northern Newport News • Socioeconomic levels are much higher than at Briarfield • A car is a virtual necessity for living in much of the area Wythe/Old Hampton (Hampton, VA) • Area consists mostly of older, well-kept, single-family houses • Socioeconomic levels are higher than in Briarfield neighborhood, and a smaller proportion relies on public assistance; therefore, relocation to a site here may represent an improvement in quality of life		

counseling services at the four sites.) The major disadvantage at Geneva Towers was the time that elapsed before a satisfactory counseling services model was worked out. Several months went by before Republic took on the counseling function itself. This prolonged process was extremely stressful for the residents.

The vouchering out of Geneva Towers could be characterized as somewhat mixed in terms of efficiency. The major glitch in the vouchering-out process was the quality of the first group of relocation counselors and their inability to coordinate activities in a competent and timely manner. Once the property management company took over the counseling function, the process became more efficient. San Francisco's usually tight housing market had eased slightly during an economic recession, and this made it easier for Geneva Towers residents to find housing than would typically have been the case.[25]

Migration Patterns

Although residents were encouraged to use relocation as an opportunity to improve and make changes in their lives, many in Baltimore and, to a lesser extent, in Kansas City and Newport News, chose to stay in the same area as their former developments.[26] In San Francisco, however, families moved twice as far as their Eutaw Gardens counterparts. The tendency of San Francisco families to make longer moves likely reflected the lack of affordable housing in the immediate vicinity of Geneva Towers.[27] These patterns are detailed below; table 2.10 summarizes the geographic aspects of the families' moves and compares destination neighborhoods.

Eutaw Gardens, Baltimore

All the Eutaw Gardens families moved either to another location in the city of Baltimore or to Baltimore County (see figure 2.1 for the location of Eutaw Gardens' 134 vouchered-out residents whose addresses could be geocoded). The average Eutaw Gardens resident moved within a radius of only two miles; only 7 percent moved more than five miles. The largest group of families, more than two-fifths (43 percent), remained in the West Baltimore area, near the location of Eutaw Gardens, many relocating to one of three mixed-income apartment buildings.[28] Others moved to more

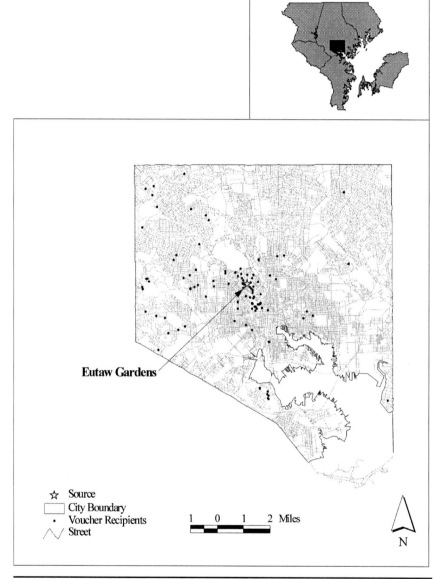

FIGURE 2.1   *Geographic distribution of voucher recipients:*
                  Eutaw Gardens, Baltimore, Maryland

Source: Center for Urban Policy Research

racially and economically diverse sections of the city, like Dickeyville-Franklintown. In many cases, the precise location governed whether the move represented an improvement in conditions for the former Eutaw Gardens residents. As a HUD housing manager noted in an interview, "It can be either really nice or pretty tough depending on what block you live on" (Kelley 1996).

Woodsong, Newport News

Most of the Woodsong families relocated into six neighborhoods when they left the site (see figure 2.2 for the location of the 287 vouchered-out residents whose addresses could be geocoded). About one-fifth of the families remained near the old site of Woodsong, moving into one of two older, but well-maintained, townhouse apartment developments. Another fifth moved deeper into the East End of Newport News, a more economically depressed area of the city with higher proportions of minorities. Nevertheless, about two-fifths moved to the northern suburban part of Newport News (an area with residents at higher socioeconomic levels)—some into older developments, but others into more modern apartment developments that had burgeoned in that part of town during the 1980s and 1990s. Finally, a fifth moved into apartment complexes and single-family homes in the neighboring city of Hampton, which a number of local informants considered a "step up" from Newport News. Whether this was the result of counseling services is hard to say.

Creston Place, Kansas City

All the Creston Place families remained in Kansas City, most staying in the same area as Creston Place or moving to nearby areas to the south or west of the development (see figure 2.3 for the location of the 34 vouchered-out residents whose addresses could be geocoded). One-third remained in the downtown area near the old development, which, despite some signs of gentrification, remained a very troubled neighborhood. A majority of housing consisted of rental units, nearly half of which were vacant. Boarded-up, abandoned shops lined commercial arteries. Another third moved to the east/central section of the city, most into a modest but adequately maintained garden apartment complex that had separate entrances to each unit and was surrounded by large open spaces. Others

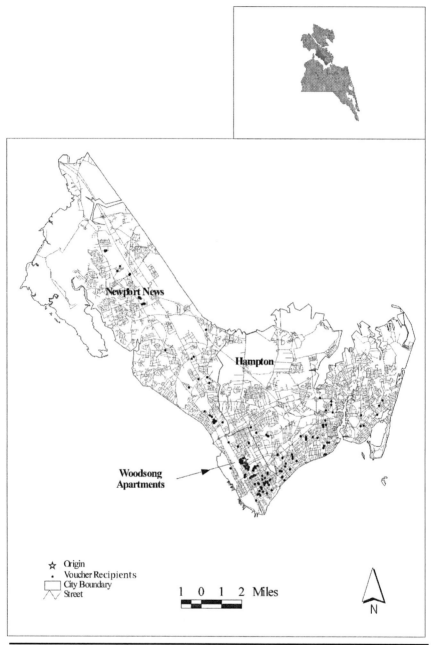

FIGURE 2.2   *Geographic distribution of voucher recipients:*
                  Woodsong Apartments, Newport News, Virginia

Source: Center for Urban Policy Research

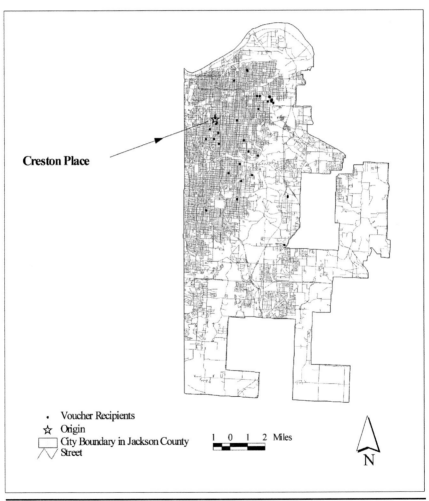

Creston Place

Voucher Recipients
Origin
City Boundary in Jackson County
Street

1 0 1 2 Miles

N

FIGURE 2.3 *Geographic distribution of voucher recipients:*
Creston Place, Kansas City, Missouri

Source: Center for Urban Policy Research

selected single-family homes that appeared to be in somewhat poor condition to accommodate their large families. Finally, a third group of former Creston Place tenants moved to older apartment buildings in the midtown/south section of the city, the location of a wide range of entertainment venues, including some adult entertainment establishments. Still, the apartment complexes were better maintained than Creston Place had been, and the city was actively working in this area on redevelopment projects.

Geneva Towers, San Francisco

For the most part, the residents of Geneva Towers relocated within the city of San Francisco, dispersing throughout the city, but about a fifth moved to other cities in the Bay Area (see figure 2.4 for the location of the vouchered-out residents). Only about one-tenth (11 percent) remained in Visitacion Valley, the site of Geneva Towers, moving into low-rise apartment complexes and single-family attached and detached homes in this stable, moderate-income, largely residential area. A larger group, or 29 percent of the Geneva Towers residents, moved to the Bayview/Hunters Point neighborhood. This neighborhood, characterized by a mix of underutilized industrial structures and older housing units, is geographically isolated from the rest of San Francisco. Its socioeconomic demographics compared unfavorably with those of Visitacion Valley—lower median household income, higher proportions of female-headed households, and high levels of unemployment. Eleven percent relocated to multifamily apartments and single-family homes in the Western Addition neighborhood, which lies in the central core of San Francisco, bordered by the Civic Center area to the east and Japantown to the north). This neighborhood presented an ethnically and socioeconomically diverse picture and was generally characterized by a relatively dense urban development pattern with parks and playgrounds interspersed throughout the urban setting. Finally, 18 percent moved elsewhere in the Bay Area, the largest number to Oakland.

Changes in Income, Property Values, and Racial Composition

In all four cities, GIS analysis confirmed that the voucher recipients' postmove neighborhoods had substantially higher income levels than their original neighborhoods (Varady and Walker 1998). The changes were particularly notable in San Francisco, where the median neighborhood income level rose from $12,300 to $29,100. House values, however, provide

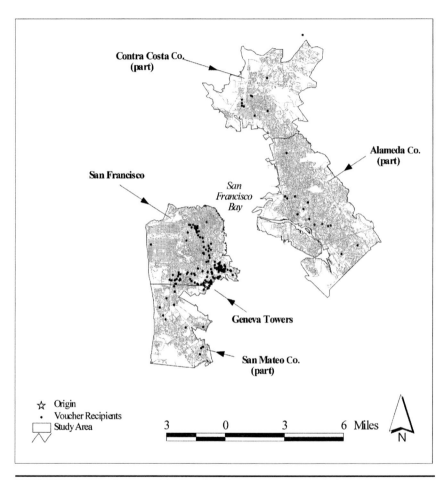

FIGURE 2.4   *Geographic distribution of voucher recipients:*
Geneva Towers, San Francisco, California

Source: Center for Urban Policy Research

more ambiguous evidence of the change in neighborhood conditions: Median house values in postmove neighborhoods (as measured by census block groups) fell below those in the original neighborhoods in Baltimore, Kansas City, and Newport News. In Baltimore, the median house value at the original location in gentrified Bolton Hill ($145,500) was more than double that in the destination neighborhoods.

The voucher recipients moved within predominantly black or racially changing corridors of the metropolitan area. As a result, when measured at the smallest unit of analysis (census block groups), overall, the recipients' postmove neighborhoods had only a marginally lower percentage of black residents. Looking at specific sites, a majority (between three-fifths and two-thirds) of Newport News, Kansas City, and San Francisco voucher recipients moved to a census tract with a proportion of blacks lower than that in their original neighborhood. However, the percentage of the population that was black in the postmove census tract usually was not appreciably lower than in the premove tract. In sharp contrast to the other three sites, only about one-tenth of Eutaw Gardens movers experienced such a change, reflecting the fact that Eutaw Gardens was located in the gentrified and racially mixed Bolton Hill community.[29]

The Residents' Experiences

For first-hand insight into the housing and neighborhood outcomes for the families, 201 former residents of the four developments were called and questioned about their experiences. How had they felt about moving? What were their experiences during the vouchering out? How satisfied were they, and how did their new housing and neighborhoods compare with their old? We found both commonalities and differences among the four sites as residents discussed their experiences with their housing search, discrimination, relocation counseling, housing choices, and changes in housing and neighborhood conditions. Below we present and compare findings for the four sites.

Leaving the Vouchered-Out Site

Given the poor conditions at the four developments, one might assume that the residents would have been eager to move, but this was not the case. Overall, one-fifth (21 percent) said that they were unhappy about moving, and a little under a third (31 percent) said that they would have preferred to stay where they were; less than half (48 percent) said that they were happy to move.

By site, however, differences were observed. Approximately three-fifths (61 percent) of the Eutaw Gardens respondents said that they were to some degree unhappy about moving, the highest proportion among the four sites (see table 2.11). At Geneva Towers, too, a majority was unhappy about moving (55 percent). At Woodsong and at Creston Place, however, most of the residents were happy to leave their troubled developments (53 and 69 percent, respectively). Conditions at these two developments were apparently worse than at Eutaw Gardens and Geneva Towers.

The results at Eutaw Gardens and Geneva Towers resemble those observed by Vale in his 1997 study of five Boston public housing developments. Although many of the Boston residents complained about crime and drugs, most said that they were satisfied with their homes and nearly half planned to remain at their locations as long as possible. Some put up with bad neighborhood conditions because they felt that they had no choice; others endured these conditions because they had friends and relatives nearby to provide help when needed.[30]

Length of Time and Scope of the Housing Search

Because of San Francisco's tight housing market (despite its slight softening before the vouchering out), it was expected that the Geneva Towers voucher recipients would spend more time looking and consider more options before they found a suitable unit than would recipients at the other sites. Survey results supported both of these assumptions. Voucher recipients in Kansas City, Newport News, and Baltimore spent between one and two months searching for suitable housing; recipients in San Francisco searched for an average of three and a half months. Similarly, San Francisco recipients needed to look at a larger number of units before finding one that was suitable (an average of nearly seven units, compared with an average of five at the other three sites).

An assumption that the vouchered-out families, like other low-income households, would confine their housing search to the same neighborhood as the distressed development or to nearby neighborhoods was not supported for the sample as a whole.[31] Only a fifth (21 percent)

TABLE 2.11

Housing Search Characteristics Compared

Characteristic	Eutaw Gardens	Woodsong	Creston Place	Geneva Towers
Feelings about moving from original location [HS]	• 61% were either unhappy about moving or preferred to stay • Those receiving AFDC were more likely to prefer to stay; unemployed were more likely to prefer to stay	• 47% were either unhappy about moving or preferred to stay • High school graduates tended to be happy to move	• 30% were either unhappy about moving or preferred to stay • *	• 55% were either unhappy about moving or preferred to stay • Long-term residents, older householders, and married ones tended to prefer to stay; households with children, householders experiencing overcrowding, and high school graduates tended to be happy to move
Length of time in housing search [HS]	• Average = 2.0 months • 22% spent 1 month or less; 35% spent more than 2 months • Households with children, those with 3 or more members, those relatively overcrowded, and those with low incomes were more likely to spend 1 or more months looking	• Average = 1.4 months • 41% spent 1 month or less; 18% spent more than 2 months • No significant differences by subgroup	• Average = 0.8 months • 54% spent 1 month or less; 0% spent more than 2 months • *	• Average = 3.5 months • 20% spent 1 month or less; 47% spent more than 2 months • Households with young children were less likely to spend 1 or more months looking
Number of places looked at in housing search	• Average = 5.1 places • 52% looked at 4 or more places • Households with children, those with 3 or more members, and those relatively overcrowded were more likely to look at 4 or more places; those 50 and older were less likely	• Average = 5.0 places • 59% looked at 4 or more places • Households with 3 or more members were more likely to look at 4 or more places; those married, those with incomes $5,000 and above, and those who had lived at the previous location for 5 years or more were less likely	• Average = 4.9 places • 46% looked at 4 or more places • *	• Average = 6.6 places • 71% looked at 4 or more places • Households with children, and those receiving AFDC were more likely to look at 4 or more places; those 50 and above were less likely

74

Geographical pattern of places considered [HS]	39% looked at near neighborhoods only; 18% looked at far ones only; 39% looked at both near and far neighborhoods • Those 50 and older were more likely to look at nearby places only; households with children, ones with 3 or more members, those relatively overcrowded, and those receiving AFDC were less likely to limit search	13% looked at near neighborhoods only; 40% looked at far ones only; 45% looked at both near and far neighborhoods • Married householders and those who had lived at location 5 years or more were more likely to look at nearby locations only; households with 3 or more members were less likely	15% looked at near neighborhoods only; 69% looked at far ones only; 15% looked at both near and far neighborhoods • *	16% looked at near neighborhoods only; 24% looked at far ones only; 53% looked at both near and far neighborhoods • Those 50 and older were more likely to look at nearby locations only; those with young children were less likely
Sources of information [HS]	Friends and relatives, "went by" building	Friends and relatives, "went by" building, listings, agency officials	Friends and relatives, †"went by" building, †listings, agency officials	Agency officials, friends and relatives, listings
Discrimination [HS]	77% reported they experienced no discrimination in their housing search • Of the 10 respondents reporting discrimination, 6 (60%) mentioned Section 8 voucher discrimination; 1 (10%) mentioned racial discrimination • Households with 3 or more members and those in relatively overcrowded units were more likely to report discrimination	67% reported they experienced no discrimination in their housing search • Of the 26 respondents reporting discrimination, 12 (46%) mentioned Woodsong's poor reputation; 5 (19%) mentioned Section 8 voucher discrimination; 3 (12%) mentioned racial discrimination • Those 50 years old and older were more likely to report discrimination; those with young children were less likely	69% reported they experienced no discrimination in their housing search • Of the 3 respondents reporting discrimination, 2 mentioned Section 8 voucher discrimination; none mentioned racial discrimination • *	78% reported they experienced no discrimination in their housing search • Of the 11 respondents reporting discrimination, 5 (46%) mentioned racial discrimination; 5 (46%) mentioned Section 8 voucher discrimination • Those with a high school degree were more likely to report discrimination
Why chose home [HS]	Location/accessibility, building conditions, safe neighborhood, limited time	Location/accessibility, limited time, safe neighborhood, †limited choice, †more space	†Limited choice, †public transportation, ††safe neighborhood, ††limited time	Location/accessibility, safe neighborhood, building conditions

(continued)

TABLE 2.11 (continued)

Characteristic	Eutaw Gardens	Woodsong	Creston Place	Geneva Towers
Satisfaction with housing search [HS]	• 57% said they were satisfied • Households with incomes $5,000 and above were less likely to be satisfied	• 68% said they were satisfied • Householders who preferred to stay at Woodsong were less likely to be satisfied	• 61% said they were satisfied • *	• 55% said they were satisfied • Householders who preferred to stay at Geneva Towers and those who received AFDC were less likely to be satisfied
Reasons for satisfaction with the housing search (among those satisfied) [HS]	Better conditions, better neighborhood, quality of assistance	Better neighborhood, quality of assistance, better conditions	Better neighborhood, better conditions	Better conditions, [†]better neighborhood, [†]quality of assistance
Reasons for dissatisfaction with the housing search (among those dissatisfied) [HS]	Wanted to stay, lack of assistance, moving difficult	Moving difficult, lack of information, wanted to stay	Home conditions, moving difficult, expenses	Wanted to stay, [†]moving difficult, [†]lack of information
Residents' awareness of counseling [HS]	• 87% aware of counseling • Those who were living under relatively crowded conditions and those who preferred to remain at Eutaw Gardens were less likely to be aware of counseling	• 66% aware of counseling • Those who preferred to stay at Woodsong were less likely to be aware of counseling.	• 39% aware of counseling	• 68% aware of counseling • Those who were not high school graduates, and those that had lived at Geneva Towers less than 5 years, were less likely to be aware of counseling
Residents' use of counseling [HS]	• 52% reported they used counseling • Employed householders were	• 36% reported they used counseling • Householders 50 and over and	[Only 1 Creston Place respondent to the survey indicated use of counseling; therefore,	• 39% reported they used counseling • Those who preferred to

	more likely to use counseling; those married, those in relatively crowded units, those who had lived at Eutaw Gardens 5 or more years, and those preferring to stay at Eutaw Gardens were less likely to use it	those preferring to stay at Woodsong were more likely to use counseling; those with children and those receiving AFDC were less likely	Creston Place results on counseling questions are not presented]	remain at Geneva Towers were more likely to use counseling
Reasons for not using counseling [HS]	Not needed; counselor ineffective; counselor unreachable	Not needed; counselor unreachable; knew too late	Not needed; counselor ineffective	Not needed; counselor ineffective; knew too late
Average number of times met with counselor [HS]	2.8	3.7	*	6.3
Types of relocation services utilized and portion of tenants receiving help with each: [HS]				
• Listing possible places to call on	61%	73%	*	65%
• Choosing neighborhoods to search in	68%	57%	*	30%
• Calculating rent	71%	80%	*	65%
• Managing household budget	50%	50%	*	25%

(continued)

TABLE 2.11 (continued)

Characteristic	Eutaw Gardens	Woodsong	Creston Place	Geneva Towers
• Dealing with family problems	11%	23%	*	10%
• Filling out HUD applications	52%	60%	*	60%
• Filling out rental applications and references	36%	37%	*	60%
• Understanding lease agreements	52%	60%	*	60%
• Setting up utility accounts	29%	30%	*	42%
• Paying for moving expenses	64%	77%	*	90%
• Understanding fair housing laws	75%	80%	*	70%
• Dealing with neighborhood/ landlord problems	37%	47%	*	20%
• Transportation to possible rentals	25%	50%	*	65%
Things liked most about counseling [HS]	Availability of counselors, †provided information, †provided listings	Availability of counselors, provided information	*	Availability of counselors, provided information

Things liked least about counseling [HS]	60% said "nothing"; "not enough help" most frequently mentioned weakness	82% said "nothing"; no complaint mentioned often enough to be meaningful	*	80% said "nothing"; no complaint mentioned often enough to be meaningful
Average number of apartments counselor suggested [HS]	7.5	7.4	*	5.7
Whether counseling influenced final decision concerning where to move [HS]	46% said counseling was important	52% said counseling was important	*	50% said counseling was important
Impact of relocation counseling on housing search [HS]	• Householders who used counseling, and particularly those who used 6 or more relocation services, were more likely to be satisfied with the search • Householders who received 8 or more suggestions tended to look at more places, but were not more likely to focus on distant locations	• Householders who met with counselor 3 or more times were less likely to be satisfied with the housing search • Householders who used counseling were more likely to spend 2 or more months looking; those who met with counselor 3 or more times were more likely to look at 4 or more places	*	• No significant associations between counseling and satisfaction with the housing search • Householders who used counseling, and particularly those who met with counselors 3 or more times, were more likely to look at 4 or more places

Note: HS refers to information derived from the household survey. * = too small a base to report crosstabular results. † = Respondents were asked a series of open-ended questions on the housing search and on satisfaction with housing conditions (e.g., the most important reason for choosing their home, the most important reason for being satisfied with their current home). In each case, they were asked about their "first most important reason," then about their "second most important reason." The open-ended questions were post-coded, resulting in three distinct variables per set. The response categories for the first variable in each set (i.e., the first most important reason) are listed in descending order based on the number of times that response category was mentioned. One dagger (†) indicates a tie between the categories in terms of the number of times a particular response was mentioned. †† = a second tie between responses.

restricted their housing search in this way; in fact, about one-third (32 percent) of the voucher recipients considered only more distant neighborhoods of the city or the suburbs in their housing search. The pattern in Baltimore, however, was different; there, two-fifths of Eutaw Gardens voucher recipients (40 percent) looked exclusively for homes in nearby sections of West Baltimore.

Discrimination and Other Impediments to Moving

Surprisingly, discrimination during the housing search was reported by only about a fourth (27 percent) of the vouchered-out residents.[32] At two of the sites, Eutaw Gardens and Creston Place, the form of discrimination mentioned most often—among the small group that reported discrimination—was against Section 8 voucher holders. There was a group of landlords who simply did not accept Section 8 vouchers:[33]

> A lot of landlords didn't want to rent to people with vouchers. The landlords I spoke with were very nice and very positive, but they didn't want Section 8 vouchers. (An employed forty-eight-year-old single man with no children—Eutaw Gardens)

Other survey respondents noted the tendency of some landlords to equate Section 8 voucher recipients with welfare recipients and to apply the usual stereotypes to them:

> Because of the voucher, people automatically thought that you were on welfare. (Thirty-two-year-old married mother of two children—Eutaw Gardens)

Baltimore informants interviewed during the study supported the voucher recipients' reports of discrimination on the basis of Section 8 status. "Discrimination based on Section 8 may be the most important form of discrimination" (Crystal 1996). However, Section 8 status per se may not have been the critical issue. Some landlords screened out people who were on welfare, had criminal records, or were not working because they were considered to be bad risks. Thus, the landlords did not exclude all Section 8 recipients, just those perceived as having problems. Some landlords were of the opinion that workers, including part-time workers, had more initiative and motivation. Nonworkers, who spent more time at home, were thought to cause excessive wear and tear on the house.

At Geneva Towers, racial discrimination and Section 8 discrimination were reported by equal numbers of voucher recipients who believed they were treated differently when looking for a place to live. By contrast, half the former Woodsong residents who reported discrimination mentioned the poor reputation of the development and their association with it (the "Woodsong" stigma) as the reason they were treated differently. "The managers of the apartment that I wanted to rent wouldn't deal with me, period, once they knew that I was from Woodsong," was a typical comment. Being able to escape the Woodsong stigma, said one informant, by moving out of the city or state was one of the primary benefits of the vouchering out.

This is not to say that racial discrimination did not occur in the four cities where the vouchering out took place. Instead, the low reported incidence of racial discrimination might have reflected a tendency of the voucher recipients to shy away from predominantly white neighborhoods and to focus their housing search instead on predominantly black areas where landlords were accustomed to and accepted a predominantly black clientele. In addition, these areas may have been more affordable.[34]

Another impediment to moving mentioned by Eutaw Gardens residents was administrative. Baltimore County required Baltimore City tenants who had been certified by the city to be recertified by the county before they could use their vouchers in the county. Some informants claimed that this recertification process (which was fully within HUD guidelines) discouraged city-to-county moves. Others claimed that the lower Section 8 payment standards in Baltimore County, as compared with payment standards in Baltimore City, had a similar effect.[35] The issue of administrative barriers was not mentioned in any of the other cities. Sizable numbers of Woodsong tenants, for example, moved to the nearby city of Hampton without difficulty; the cooperation of the Hampton Redevelopment and Housing Authority facilitated this move.

Sources of Information

Thirty-three percent of the voucher recipients found out about their new homes through friends and relatives.[36] A slightly smaller, but still meaningful, proportion (22 percent) learned about their new unit from a relocation counselor or another housing official. Similar proportions cited "ads" (e.g., newspaper advertisements, real estate listings, listings by landlords)

(24 percent) and "going by the building" (21 percent) as their source of information. In contrast to the other three sites, Geneva Towers recipients relied more on agency officials (relocation counselors or SFHA and HUD staff) to find their new home and less on friends and walking or driving through neighborhoods. San Francisco's tight housing market may have been the reason.

Relocation Counseling

Relocation counseling at the case study sites appears to have had a limited impact on the scope of the housing search. Only about half (49 percent) of the respondents who used counseling services reported that counseling had been a somewhat or very important influence on where they looked for housing. Furthermore, relatively few tenants reported that they found out about their house or apartment from agency officials, including relocation counselors (23 percent). As mentioned above, they were more likely to find out about their new home from friends or relatives or by using the newspaper or real estate listings.

Choosing a New Home

As might be expected, in choosing their new home, the largest proportion of voucher recipients (43 percent) at all four sites sought to maximize housing quality or to find housing in a safe neighborhood. They also emphasized accessibility, with approximately one-third (32 percent) citing a desire to remain close to friends and relatives, their children's schools, and their church. Because so few tenants had a car, many also needed to be close to public transportation. As a COIL housing counselor at Eutaw Gardens noted:

> Most of the residents that I dealt with, they wanted to stay in the city. It is because of accessibility, getting around. They get around on the bus. If they moved out, farther out, it would be a little difficult to move around. If they moved close to where they were, if their church or their children's school was nearby, they maintained them in it.

A substantial minority (25 percent) of the voucher recipients said that they chose their new home by default, that is, because of "limited choice" or "limited time." Some of these recipients procrastinated, while others started early enough but ran into difficulties that prevented them from finding a more suitable home (e.g., lack of transportation to visit alternative units).

According to informants, these factors all contributed to the voucher recipients' making short-distance moves: the voucher recipients' desire to remain close to their support systems (friends, relatives, church); their tendency to look mainly in familiar areas, their reliance on the lists they were given of landlords willing to accommodate Section 8 voucher families (often landlords located in nearby areas); and a fear of discrimination, which caused recipients to focus on "safe" familiar areas (see the subsection above titled "Migration Patterns"). Kansas City informants also stressed the time constraint placed upon residents there, which meant limited assistance to move into less-known neighborhoods located farther away.

Satisfaction with the Housing Search

A majority (61 percent) of the voucher recipients surveyed at the four sites were satisfied with the housing search process. "The people who helped us relocate did very well." "They were efficient and helped a lot." These comments by Woodsong residents were typical of those made by the vouchered-out residents of all four developments. Not surprisingly, a significantly higher proportion of those who were unhappy about leaving their former homes, compared with those who wanted to leave, were dissatisfied with the housing search (48 percent compared with 28 percent).

Typically, the voucher recipients were satisfied with their housing search because their new housing and neighborhood represented a significant improvement in their quality of life. Nearly one-half (46 percent) of those who stated that they were satisfied with the housing search cited their sense of safety or the convenience of the new location. Smaller proportions cited better housing conditions (31 percent) or the quality of the relocation assistance (23 percent).

Among the minority who were dissatisfied with the housing search, nearly three-fifths (57 percent) complained about being forced to move or about the difficulty of the move. A little more than one-fourth (28 percent) cited a lack of relocation assistance, including a lack of information. Far smaller numbers complained about their new home or neighborhood (10 percent) or about discrimination based on Section 8 status (5 percent).

Housing and Neighborhood Satisfaction

Our working hypothesis—that because families would make short-distance moves, they would be dissatisfied with their new home/neighborhood and would report little improvement in their housing conditions—was not supported. In reality, four-fifths (80 percent) of the recipients were somewhat or very satisfied with their new home, and approximately two-thirds (68 percent) of the recipients reported that they were more satisfied with their new home than with the home in their previous development.[37] The remaining one-third was equally divided between those who were as satisfied and those who were less satisfied than they were with their original home. Table 2.12 shows the site-specific results dealing with housing/neighborhood satisfaction and perceived changes in residential conditions.

Given the distressed conditions of their former quarters, it is not surprising that most residents mentioned "better housing conditions" as the main reason they were more satisfied with their current home. A forty-four-year-old married woman with no children who had lived in Eutaw Gardens typified those who were pleased with the better conditions at their new homes, which at least in part were attributable to more responsive management:

> At Eutaw Gardens they had rats running around outside, sewerage back-ups, no hot water sometimes when I woke up, and leaking roofs at my place. Now I have none of those things where I am. They come around and keep the property up; everything is clean; they do inspections and spray for roaches and mice. They did not do this on a regular basis at Eutaw Gardens.

For recipients living in townhouses or single-family homes, having a private entrance was mentioned as a source of satisfaction. A former Woodsong resident, the mother of two children, said, "I don't have to walk through a hallway; I don't have to worry about people setting their trash out in the hall. Here I have a front door and a back door. No one lives over me." Others liked the play areas for their children in their new homes and neighborhoods.

Survey results about neighborhood satisfaction closely paralleled those dealing with housing satisfaction. Eighty-five percent were somewhat or very satisfied with their new neighborhood. Also, the overwhelming majority of householders (69 percent) were more satisfied with their new neighborhood than with their previous one; 19 percent were as satisfied, and 12 percent were less satisfied.

Eutaw Gardens, Creston Place, and Geneva Towers residents attributed their greater satisfaction with their new location to an enhanced sense of safety (better police protection; not having to worry about letting the children out to play) and to the restricted access to their apartment or house:

> My current neighborhood is safer than Eutaw Gardens. There are no persons standing around on corners. It just seems to me to be safer, like a family atmosphere. They watch your place when you leave; it seems homier here than at Eutaw. (A thirty-eight-year-old single working mother of two)

Former Woodsong residents particularly emphasized less noise as an improvement. They stressed the "quiet and peaceful" environment and the fact that people "didn't hang around outside." "Quiet" was equated with safety for many of the Woodsong residents. One middle-aged respondent commented, "I don't have crime here; it's very quiet." Another woman, the mother of five children, said, "At night at Woodsong, when I went to bed, there was the sound of gunfire. . . . Here, we don't have it."

Housing and Neighborhood Conditions

Objective results provide additional evidence of improvements in housing conditions. First, 40 percent of the voucher recipients interviewed in the household survey were able to move from an apartment building to a single-family attached or detached house. (At Creston Place, 70 percent of those responding to the survey moved to single-family housing; at Woodsong, 50 percent; at Geneva Towers, 40 percent; and at Eutaw Gardens, 30 percent.) This type of shift generally represents an improvement in quality of life.[38] Second, many recipients were able to obtain housing with more space, as indicated by a reported increase in the average number of rooms (from 4.93 to 5.79), and a decrease in the ratio of persons to rooms (from 0.55 to 0.49).

The evidence related to housing costs is more mixed. At one site— Eutaw Gardens—average rents dropped; at two—Woodsong and Creston Place—rents, which had been very low to start with, rose somewhat. Although the rents remained virtually the same at the fourth site—Geneva Towers—relocation did create some financial stress among Geneva Towers voucher recipients. Postmove housing costs for about half of the tenants accounted for 25 percent or more of their income. In contrast,

TABLE 2.12

Housing and Neighborhood Characteristics Compared

Characteristic	Eutaw Gardens	Woodsong	Creston Place	Geneva Towers
Satisfaction with new housing [HS]	• 83% were satisfied with new home • Married householders and those living at previous location 5 years or more were more likely to be very satisfied with new home	• 80% were satisfied with new home • Householders 50 years and older were more likely to be very satisfied with new home	• 77% were satisfied with new home • No significant differences by subgroup	• 77% were satisfied with new home • No significant differences by subgroup
Comparison of quality of old and new housing units [HS]	• 67% were more satisfied with new home • Households with young children tended to be more satisfied with their new home; those who preferred to stay at Eutaw Gardens tended to be less satisfied	• 63% were more satisfied with new home • High school graduates tended to be more satisfied with the new home; those who preferred to stay at Woodsong tended to be less satisfied	• 69% were more satisfied with new home • *	• 68% were more satisfied with new home • High school graduates and those with an income of $5,000 and above tended to be more satisfied; those who preferred to remain at Geneva Towers tended to be less satisfied
Why current home is better [HS]	• Unit in better condition, safer neighborhood, better neighborhood	• Unit in better condition, better neighborhood, †larger unit, †safer neighborhood	• Unit in better condition, safer neighborhood, larger unit	• Unit in better condition, †better neighborhood, †larger unit, safer neighborhood
Housing type[a] at new location [HS]	• Large apartment building (33%); medium-sized apartment building (22%); single-family attached house (21%) • Householders with children, particularly young children, and households with 3 or more	• Small apartment building (34%); single-family attached home (32%); single-family detached house (18%) • Households with children were more likely to move into a house	• Single-family detached home (62%); medium-sized apartment building (15%); large apartment building (15%) • *	• Small apartment building (31%); single-family attached house (20%); single-family detached house (20%); medium-sized apartment building (19%) • Households with children, those with a relatively high degree of

	members were more likely to move into a detached or attached single-family house			overcrowding, and with 3 or more members were more likely to move into a house; those who preferred to stay at Geneva Towers were less likely to move into a house
Housing cost burden (ratio of rent/income): proportion with rent/income ratio of 25% or more at new location [HS]	• 17% • Employed householders were more likely to experience a high rent cost burden	• 20% • Households with children, those with 3 or more members, those experiencing overcrowding, and those not receiving AFDC were less likely to experience a high rent cost burden	• 8% • *	• 49% • Households with incomes below $5,000 and householders 50 years and older were more likely to experience a high rent cost burden
Change in rental costs [HS]	• Average rent decreased from $143.52 to $130.06	• Average rent increased from $37.58 to $80.25	• Average rent increased from $21.92 to $81.54	• Average rent decreased from $226.60 to $222.18
Proportion experiencing an increase or decrease in rent [HS]	• Rents increased for 31% and decreased for 65% • Employed householders and those living at Eutaw Gardens 5 or more years were more likely to experience rent increases; those receiving public assistance were less likely to experience increases	• Rents increased for 54% and decreased for 21% • No significant differences by subgroup	• Rents increased for 54% and decreased for 31% • *	• Rents increased for 50% and decreased for 44% • No significant differences by subgroup

(continued)

TABLE 2.12 (continued)

Characteristic	Eutaw Gardens	Woodsong	Creston Place	Geneva Towers
Change in the number of rooms [HS]	• Average number of rooms increased from 4.7 to 5.4 • Households with children, and those with 3 or more members, were more likely to experience an increase in the number of rooms; those preferring to remain at Eutaw Gardens, and those who were age 50 and older, were less likely to experience an increase	• Average number of rooms increased from 5.1 to 5.8 • No significant differences by subgroup	• Average number of rooms increased from 4.3 to 6.5 • *	• Average number of rooms increased from 5.0 to 6.0 • Households with children, those with 3 or more members, and those experiencing over-crowding were more likely to experience an increase in the number of rooms; householders 50 years and older, those who lived at their previous location 5 years or more, and those who preferred to remain at Geneva Towers were less likely
Change in the ratio of persons/rooms [HS]	• Average decreased slightly from 0.47 to 0.44 • Households with children, those with 3 or more members and those relatively overcrowded at Eutaw Gardens tended to experience an increase in space; those 50 years and older, and those who preferred to stay at Eutaw Gardens, were less likely to obtain more space	• Average decreased slightly from 0.55 to 0.50 • Households with 3 or more members were more likely to experience a decrease in overcrowding	• Average decreased slightly from 0.68 to 0.52 • Households with 3 or more members were more likely to experience an increase in space	• Average decreased from 0.61 to 0.50 • Households with children, those with 3 or more members, those experiencing a relatively high degree of overcrowding at Geneva Towers, and those receiving AFDC obtained more space; householders 50 and older were less likely to obtain more space

Satisfaction with new neighborhood [HS]	• 83% were satisfied with new neighborhood • Households that had lived at Eutaw Gardens 5 years or more and did not prefer to stay were more likely to be very satisfied	• 88% were satisfied with new neighborhood • Those householders 50 years and older and high school graduates were more likely to be very satisfied; those who preferred to stay at Woodsong were less likely to be very satisfied	• 85% were satisfied with new neighborhood • *	• 82% were satisfied with new neighborhood • Employed householders were less likely to be very satisfied with new neighborhood
Comparison of quality of old and new neighborhoods [HS]	• 63% were more satisfied with new neighborhood • Those who preferred to stay at Eutaw Gardens were less likely to be more satisfied with new neighborhood	• 69% were more satisfied with new neighborhood • Those who preferred to stay at Woodsong were less likely to be more satisfied with new neighborhood	• 61% were more satisfied with new neighborhood • *	• 78% were more satisfied with new neighborhood • No significant differences by subgroup
Reasons why current neighborhood is better [HS]	• Safety, †neighbors, †atmosphere	• Atmosphere, †neighbors, †safety	• Safety, fewer drugs	• Safety, atmosphere, fewer drugs
Perception of safety at new location [HS]	• 78% felt safe at new location • No significant differences by subgroup	• 87% felt safe at new location • No significant differences by subgroup	• 85% felt safe at new location • *	• 84% felt safe at new location • No significant differences by subgroup
Comparison of safety at old and new neighborhoods [HS]	• 55% felt safer at new location • Employed householders were more likely to feel safer at new neighborhood; those receiving public assistance and those preferring to stay at Eutaw Gardens were less likely to feel safer	• 59% felt safer at new location • High school graduates were more likely to feel safer; those with young children and those preferring to remain at Woodsong were less likely to feel safer	• 54% felt safer at new location • *	• 59% felt safer at new location • No significant differences by subgroup

(continued)

TABLE 2.12 (continued)

Characteristic	Eutaw Gardens	Woodsong	Creston Place	Geneva Towers
Accessibility of new site to: [HS]				
• Job opportunities	• 22% said accessibility to job opportunities was better	• 26% said accessibility to job opportunities was better	• 9% said accessibility to job opportunities was better	• 31% said accessibility to job opportunities was better
• Schools	• 18% said availability of good schools was better	• 34% said availability of good schools was better	• 46% said availability of good schools was better	• 29% said availability of good schools was better
• Shopping	• 43% said availability of good shopping was better	• 37% said availability of good shopping was better	• 46% said availability of good shopping was better	• 53% said availability of good shopping was better
• Friends	• 38% said ability to see friends was better	• 55% said ability to see friends was better	• 46% said ability to see friends was better	• 52% said ability to see friends was better
• Doctors	• 23% said ability to see doctors was better	• 17% said ability to see doctors was better	• 8% said ability to see doctors was better	• 27% said ability to see doctors was better
	• Overall, greatest improvements occurred in availability of good shopping and in ability to see friends	• Overall, greatest improvements occurred in ability to see friends and in availability of good shopping	• Overall, greatest improvements occurred in availability of good schools, availability of good shopping, and in ability to see friends	• Overall, greatest improvements occurred in availability of good shopping and ability to see friends
Perceptions of neighborhood strengths [HS]	• 52% cited 3 or more neighborhood items as better at new location	• 52% cited 3 or more neighborhood items as better at new location	• 46% cited 3 or more neighborhood items as better at new location	• 61% cited 3 or more neighborhood items as better at new location

90

Proportion perceiving three or more items as better at new location [HS]	• No significant differences by subgroup	• Households with young children and those who preferred to remain at Woodsong were less likely to cite 3 or more neighborhood items as better	• *	• Larger families were less likely to cite 3 or more items as better
Changes in employment status [HS]	9% became employed after the move, but 13% became unemployed; the remainder stayed the same	10% became employed; 5% became unemployed	31% became employed; 8% became unemployed	18% became employed; 2% became unemployed
Proportion receiving AFDC (post-move) [HS]	• 39%	• 47%	• 31%	• 35%
Interest in moving from current location [HS]	• 44% were interested in moving • Householders living at Eutaw Gardens 5 years or more were less likely to want to move	• 64% were interested in moving • Householders 50 years and older were less likely to want to move	• 66% were interested in moving • *	• 44% were interested in moving • Households with children, those with 3 or more members, and employed household heads were more likely to want to move; those 50 years and older were less likely to want to move

Note: HS refers to information derived from the household survey. *Too small a base to report crosstabular results. † Respondents were asked a series of open-ended questions on the housing search and on satisfaction with housing conditions (e.g., the most important reason for choosing their home, the most important reason for being satisfied with their current home). In each case, they were asked about their "first most important reason," then about their "second most important reason." The open-ended questions were post-coded, resulting in three distinct variables per set. The response categories for the first variable in each set (i.e., the first most important reason) are listed in descending order based on the number of times that response category was mentioned. One dagger (†) indicates a tie between the categories in terms of the number of times a particular response was mentioned.
Apartment building size: Small, 2 to 4 units; medium-sized, 5 to 9 units; large, 10 or more units.

although many Eutaw Gardens voucher recipients experienced increases in out-of-pocket housing costs, less than 20 percent had such a high housing-cost burden. The difference between Geneva Towers and the other sites undoubtedly reflects the tighter San Francisco housing market, where, even with higher subsidies, residents have to pay more for rent to find decent housing.

Overall, most of the voucher recipients (84 percent) reported that they felt safe near their new homes.[39] Within this group, almost half (47 percent) said that they felt very safe. Almost three-fifths (57 percent) of the respondents reported that they felt safer at their new location than at their original one. Thirty-one percent felt about as safe, while the remaining 12 percent felt less safe. Some said that they were less afraid of shootings and other forms of violence. Others attributed their feeling of safety to better neighbors who "cared more" and who were more vigilant, to block-watch groups, and to the presence of homeowners.

In the survey, the voucher recipients were also asked to what extent the move had affected their access to job opportunities, schools, shopping, friends, doctors, and medical services. Because many recipients remained in the same or nearby neighborhoods after moving to their new home, only minor changes were to be expected. This turned out to be the case (see table 2.13). The availability of shopping and the ability to see friends were improvements mentioned by approximately 50 percent of all respondents. Far fewer reported improvements in the other aspects of accessibility.

Moving Desires

Given the high levels of housing and neighborhood satisfaction, it might seem surprising that more than half (52 percent) of the respondents wanted to move again. Some of those wanting to move again complained about some unsatisfactory aspect of their new home or neighborhood (e.g., inadequate heat, a landlord who did not make needed repairs, loud music, drug dealing). However, for many of the respondents who wanted to move again, the vouchers appeared to have broadened their horizons. They now wanted something better, or a house instead of an apartment. Others, like the former Woodsong resident below, were satisfied with their new home but hoped to move again to a unit more closely approximating their housing ideal:

TABLE 2.13

Comparison of Neighborhood Conditions before and after Being Vouchered Out

	Rating			
Attribute	*Better*	*About the Same*	*Worse*	*N =* [a]
Job opportunities	24.6%	70.5%	4.9%	142
Availability of good schools	29.7%	64.8%	5.5%	145
Availability of good shopping	43.2%	45.2%	11.6%	199
Ability to see friends	49.0%	41.4%	9.6%	198
Ability to see doctors	20.4%	73.0%	6.6%	196

[a] "Don't knows" have been excluded from the analysis.

[I want to move] because I couldn't go where I wanted to go at the time, the place that I really wanted. The place wasn't ready at the time, but the place is ready now. Nothing really is wrong with the place that I'm living in; however, I really liked the place that wasn't ready at the time....[It] is in a part of the town where I want to be. (A 36-year-old single mother with one child)

Self-Sufficiency

It would have been unrealistic to expect that many unemployed voucher recipients would have found jobs in conjunction with relocation. Relocation counselors placed little emphasis on family self-sufficiency. Furthermore, because many recipients made only short-distance moves, accessibility to jobs should not have been affected. Looking at the specific sites, most Eutaw Gardens residents experienced no change in employment status; the number who became employed was more than balanced by the number who became unemployed. The results at the other sites were more positive. Although majorities at these sites experienced no change in employment status,[40] more did become employed than became unemployed. Because of the relatively small sample sizes, however, extreme caution should be exercised in interpreting the somewhat positive results at three of the four sites. Further research is needed before any conclusions can be drawn with respect to the employment effects of vouchering out on individuals.

What Types of Householders Were Most Likely to Be Satisfied with Their New Homes?

The multiple regression results (tables 2.3 through 2.6) provide mixed support for the hypothesis that those who used the relocation counseling services would conduct more effective housing searches and would be the ones who were most satisfied with their new home. In fact, those who took advantage of relocation counseling were not more likely to be very satisfied with their home than those who knew about the services but did not use them. It is likely that the householders who were aware of the services but did not use them were the more energetic ones in the sample and were savvy about the housing market. These traits enabled them to do as well as tenants who took advantage of the different types of counseling services.[41] The householders who were unaware of the relocation services, however, were significantly less likely to be very satisfied with their home compared with the householders who used them.[42] Those who were unaware of services were probably the more unsophisticated home seekers, and the lack of sophistication may have led to less effective housing searches.

Contrary to expectations, distance played no significant role in explaining variations in satisfaction when other characteristics were controlled. The insignificant result probably reflects three factors. First, the vouchering-out pattern at Geneva Towers was somewhat unique. Geneva Towers was located in Visitacion Valley at the southern edge of San Francisco, and not in the inner city. Because this area had a high home-ownership rate and a low incidence of crime, short-distance moves within the neighborhood led to the highest levels of housing satisfaction.[43]

Second, as suggested by Homer Hoyt's sector theory (Knox 1994, 101), cities can best be understood in terms of sectors defined by transportation routes and topography; these sectors are relatively homogeneous in social class. One sector might be occupied primarily by the middle class, another by the working class, and a third by the low-income class. The theory implies that if one draws radii from the center to delineate different sectors, neighborhood and housing quality would vary more by sector than by distance from the center. Or, to state the point somewhat differently, households at the same distance from the vouchered-out development, but in different sectors, would experience considerable differences in neighborhood quality.

Third, there is likely to be considerable variation of quality within neighborhoods regardless of distance from the original development. Housing abandonment, drugs, and gangs may be serious problems on one block, whereas conditions may be considerably better a few blocks away. Thus, low-income voucher recipients who wanted to both remain close to the location of their original developments and still improve their living conditions may have been able to do so by making relatively short-distance moves.

As expected, residents who were happy to leave the vouchered-out development were more likely to be satisfied with the new home than were either those who were willing to move but who preferred to stay or those who were happy about moving. The cross-tabular results highlighted a big difference in satisfaction between those unhappy about moving and members of the other two groups: those who preferred to stay but were willing to move, and those who were happy after moving. Thirty-five percent of those who were unhappy about moving were very satisfied with their new home. In contrast, 57 percent of those who preferred to stay (but who were willing to move) and 54 percent of those who were happy about moving were very satisfied with their new home. The path analysis results show that being happy to leave the vouchered-out complex led to an increased likelihood of being very satisfied with one's new home. However, because the effect was indirect, through satisfaction with the housing search, the total effect was modest (0.07).

Most of the remaining multiple regression results were as expected. Those who moved into a house, who were very satisfied with the housing search, and who felt very safe at their current location were most likely to be very satisfied with their current home. The fact that the unemployed were more likely to be dissatisfied with their home may have been due to these householders being dissatisfied with life in general. Similarly, those who were married were more likely to be satisfied with their home than single householders, perhaps because of their overall satisfaction with life. It is unclear why those receiving public assistance were more likely to be satisfied with their new home than those not dependent on welfare.

Surprisingly, a high rent-to-income ratio (i.e., 50 percent and above) was associated with housing satisfaction, but there may be a fairly simple explanation. Voucher recipients can choose homes with rents exceeding the local authority's payment standard if the householder is willing to pay the extra amount out-of-pocket. It is possible that the voucher recipients who made the decision to pay the extra amount in return for living in units that closely matched their needs were very satisfied with their choices.

A priori, we had no reason to expect that a Newport News location would affect housing satisfaction one way or the other. However, this factor had a strong negative impact on housing satisfaction. The Newport News respondents were also more likely than those at the other sites to want to move again. These results are hard to explain given the informant interviews, which suggested that the counseling provided by an out-of-town professional encouraged tenants to carry out a more wide-ranging search than would otherwise have been the case—a search method that, presumably, would result in better choices. In fact, the counselor had tried to steer people in their housing choices, but she found that some residents had other ideas:

> I wanted them [the residents] to move in the better areas because, to me, that's the whole purpose of using your voucher—it's to get into better areas. But, to my dismay, a lot of people wanted to stay close. So, I had...to kind of backtrack and say, "OK, I'll look into these type places because that's where you want to go." (Williams 1996)

Many of the former Woodsong residents reporting "no change" in housing or other conditions had stayed in the neighborhood near Woodsong. The open-ended responses to the survey suggest, however, that although some Newport News voucher recipients disliked their new homes and neighborhoods because of problems with the units and the prevalence of crime, many others expressed dissatisfaction not for negative reasons but because they viewed their home as a stepping-stone to something better. It is not clear, however, why the Newport News relocatees had less of an attachment to their new location than the relocatees in the other three cities.

Conclusions

The Gautreaux Housing Program and the Moving to Opportunity Demonstration Program have produced notable results—improvements in employment for participants, increases in educational attainment for the children—but the findings may reflect key program features not found in the regular Section 8 program, that is, a reliance on volunteers, intensive counseling, and geographical restrictions on where families can move. The question that we have attempted to answer in this chapter is: How will families involuntarily displaced from distressed federally subsidized housing fare if provided with a housing voucher and moderate counseling but no restrictions on where they can move? How many residents will take advantage of moderate counseling? How far will residents move, and how successful will these moves be? Will residents be able to improve their housing and neighborhood conditions?

This chapter has sought to answer these questions through an analysis of the experiences of households relocated from four distressed developments in Baltimore, Newport News, Kansas City, and San Francisco. Although residents were encouraged to use relocation as an opportunity to improve their lives, many in Baltimore, Kansas City, and Newport News chose to stay in the same area.

Despite the short distance of many moves, most voucher recipients improved their situation by moving. The overwhelming majority were satisfied with their new home and neighborhood; most said that they were more satisfied with their new home and neighborhood than they had been in their former situation. Many attributed their greater satisfaction to an enhanced sense of security and safety, due in part to more restricted entryways to the house or apartment, more vigilant neighbors, and better police protection. The fact that two-fifths of the respondents were able to move from an apartment to a house is itself evidence of improvement.

Although most voucher recipients were satisfied with their new locations, many had only weak attachments. More than half reported that they would like to move again if they could. Surprisingly, many who said that they were satisfied with their current home also wished to move. Some of these families felt they had been pressured to move too quickly from the vouchered-out development and, as a result, had been unable to find a unit that was "just right" and had settled for a "satisfactory" one. Many of these householders now wanted to conduct a more thorough housing search. Others reported that though they were happy with their current unit, they wanted a larger home, a single-family house, and/or one with more amenities (e.g., a larger yard, or central air conditioning). Thus, the large proportion wishing to move did not necessarily indicate a failure on the part of the vouchering-out process or in the use of vouchers. Many wished to move in order to more closely approximate their housing ideal. It is quite possible that many of those who stayed close to their old developments in conjunction with vouchering out will move farther away to lower-poverty neighborhoods in succeeding moves.

The results provide inconclusive and somewhat contradictory evidence on how much (if at all) relocation counseling contributed to the improvements in housing and neighborhood conditions. Just half the respondents who claimed to have used counseling reported that it had been important to them in the housing search. The results also indicate that the families that participated in relocation counseling were not significantly more likely to conduct an intensive or geographically broad search, to be satisfied with the search, or to be very satisfied with their new location. The fact that those that were unaware of counseling services did worst in terms of housing satisfaction is worth noting. These householders may have lacked the motivation or savvy to take advantage of services. Both factors would have hurt them in their housing search. More sophisticated outreach efforts may be required to help these people.

The results dealing with intracity variations in housing search methods and housing satisfaction were somewhat mixed. Because of San Francisco's tight housing market, residents moved farther from the vouchered-out site. However, in contrast to what was anticipated, it was in Newport News, not in San Francisco, that the results showed a reduced likelihood of voucher recipients being very satisfied, when other factors were controlled. Analysis of the open-ended responses to the survey, however, indicated that many former Woodsong residents now wanted to "try something different" or to "move up" within the housing stock into a single-family home. Having made the first move, voucher recipients may have viewed a second move as less daunting.

The fact that so many residents were able to improve their housing conditions within the context of short moves can be explained in several ways. First, because conditions were poor at the four distressed developments, voucher recipients could only improve their housing situation by moving into units that met Section 8 standards. In addition, crime, abandoned buildings, and other indicators of decline often varied sharply within the neighborhoods containing the distressed developments. Consequently, a relatively short move from the development could represent a large improvement. Furthermore, the demolition of these distressed developments resulted in improving the social and physical conditions of the neighborhoods. Finally, the fact that many voucher recipients were able to stay near their friends and relatives and close to dense public transportation networks contributed to their satisfaction with the search and with their new location.

Although, in general, housing and neighborhood conditions improved as a result of the move, most families continued to live in racially segregated areas. In all four cities, the voucher recipients moved within predominantly black or racially changing corridors of the metropolitan area. Measured at the smallest unit of analysis (census block group), the recipients' postmove neighborhoods had only a marginally lower percentage of African-American residents.

The above findings suggest that in many cities it may be unreasonable to expect many voucher recipients who move involuntarily—particularly those relying on public transportation—to relocate to new and unfamiliar neighborhoods without support or without energetic counseling encouraging them to do so. Further, because some of the case study sites were not in inner-city slums but in decent residential areas, the tendency of many voucher recipients to remain in the original vicinity should not be regarded as an indication that the vouchering-out process was unsuccessful. The very demolition of the developments provided substantial neighborhood improvement, and a large majority of the residents were content with their new homes.

Notes

1. In Section 8 "counseling," housing authority staff meet with applicants in group sessions, distribute published information (e.g., listings of landlords renting to Section 8 tenants, tenants' rights under fair housing laws), and provide help in answering questions and completing forms. Counselors generally do meet individually with applicants to determine their income eligibility; however, whether these sessions constitute counseling is debatable.

2. Involuntary movers did not want to move but were eventually forced to relocate; voluntary movers either voluntarily chose to move to scattered-site public housing or used a special mobility certificate that required them to move to a low-poverty area.

3. We assumed that if half or more of the respondents said that they were dissatisfied with their new home and neighborhood, this would constitute a relatively high level of dissatisfaction.

4. Conversely, it seemed equally plausible to us that because conditions were so poor in the vouchered-out developments, even a short move with a housing voucher could lead to improvements in housing and neighborhood conditions.

5. The research plan called for interviews with 200 families; an additional interview was conducted with an individual who responded to our "800" number after our goal of 200 interviews had been reached and was included in the survey, for a total of 201 interviews.

6. We included "help in deciding the neighborhood to search in" in the housing search scale, rather than the budgeting scale, even though the item loaded higher in the budgeting scale. Logically, the item seemed to fit better in the search scale. Furthermore, by including this item in the search scale, we were increasing the possible degree of variation.

7. The regressions were run in three stages. First, the determinants of housing satisfaction were examined, including objective background characteristics, use of relocation counseling, components of the housing search, satisfaction with the housing search, and perceived safety. The regression analysis utilized a dichotomized recoding scheme for housing satisfaction that distinguished between those householders who were less than fully satisfied and those who were fully satisfied with their housing unit. Second, testing was done for the determinants of satisfaction with the housing search, and assessments of neighborhood safety. Third, the determinants of different components of the housing search (e.g., whether the respondent restricted the search to the same neighborhood as the vouchering-out site or to nearby neighborhoods) were examined. We were careful to restrict the latter analysis to background factors that could logically have affected the search. Thus, we included employment status at the time of moving out of the distressed development, and happiness about leaving, but left out current employment status and socioeconomic indicators for the new neighborhood (e.g., median household income level). These three sets of regression analyses were run separately for the total sample (where we included dummy variables identifying householders unaware of counseling and those aware of counseling services but who did not use them) and for the counseled sample (where we included the summated scales measuring use of the four types of counseling services).

8. In the path diagrams, the hypothesized causal relationships were represented by unidirectional arrows extending from each determining variable to each dependent variable. Standardized regression coefficients were placed on the unidirectional arrows and provide evidence of the relative importance of the independent variables. Tables 2.4 and 2.5 summarize the information in the path diagrams by indicating the indirect, direct, and total effects of the variables. In order to measure the indirect effects, it was necessary to compute the effects of background characteristics through the paths portrayed in the diagrams. The results from the separate indirect paths were added to compute the total indirect effects. The total effect for each variable was obtained by adding the direct and the indirect effects.

9. The final case study sites were geographically diverse; included sites with tight (San Francisco) and open (Newport News) housing markets; were among the largest developments (with the exception of Kansas City); and contained no

unique conditions that would limit the usefulness of the findings (Puerto Rico, for example, was eliminated on this basis).

10. Ninety-four percent of the householders were black; the remaining 6 percent of the householders were fairly equally distributed among whites, Asians, Hispanics, and others. Eighty-six percent were women. Seventy-nine percent were not married (i.e., they were divorced, or separated, or had never been married).

11. Pressure from Bolton Hill and Madison Park residents played an important part in HUD's decision to close Eutaw Gardens.

12. Compared with the other sites, among those surveyed, Eutaw Gardens contained the highest proportion of households without children (46 percent). Creston Place in Kansas City contained the highest proportion of household heads that worked (70 percent). Geneva Towers in San Francisco contained the lowest proportion of black tenants (82 percent), the highest proportion who were married or widowed (40 percent), and the highest proportion who had lived at the site five years or more (90 percent). (See table 2.2.) Compared with Section 8 voucher recipients nationwide at that time (*Recent Research Results* 1995), the vouchered-out residents were more likely to be black, under 25 years old, and on public assistance. In addition, they had higher incomes and paid less rent than voucher recipients nationally.

13. COIL had estimated that 125 households would use counseling. This turned out to be very close to the actual number (127). This number is smaller than the number (161) of households that relocated from Eutaw Gardens. The discrepancy includes families that moved without counseling; some of these families relocated before COIL began its operation. "They had taken care of everything that needed to be done. Through ARCO, they had gotten their security deposit taken care of, utilities, everything, the voucher from the city to move. They did not need counseling. There are always a few that don't want it" (Iber 1996).

14. This does not mean that all inner-city neighborhood nonprofit organizations are antisuburban. However, it does mean that many community leaders, like the two agency directors interviewed in Baltimore, are less than enthusiastic about housing mobility efforts, which they see undercutting inner-city renewal.

15. During the time Eutaw Gardens was being vouchered out, (1) the Housing Authority of Baltimore City (HABC) was being criticized almost daily in the newspapers for the poor administration of its voucher and housing subsidy programs; (2) the city's MTO program was being resisted by residents and politicians in Baltimore County; and (3) the American Civil Liberties Union was suing HABC on the grounds that the agency's public housing was racially and economically segregated, and it was recommending that public housing residents be given vouchers to use in low-poverty/low-minority areas.

16. The broader Hampton Roads area covers almost 1,700 square miles and includes nine independent cities (Norfolk among them) and six counties.

17. At a press conference announcing a crackdown on such landlords in

1997, HUD Secretary Andrew Cuomo and Attorney General Janet Reno stood next to a photograph of a Woodsong apartment.

18. SWAT was a team comprised of HUD field officers whose mission was to take action against owners of federally subsidized housing developments who failed to keep their properties up to HUD standards. Its functions were taken over by HUD's Enforcement Center in 1998.

19. These ranged from one-to-one counseling to delinquent debt assistance, deposit/utilities assistance, referrals to community resources, locating available and affordable housing, locating larger units, conducting workshops on search techniques, dealing with the stress of moving, and transporting residents to look for housing.

20. Estimates of new landlords were provided by the Newport News and the Hampton housing authorities.

21. As we shall see later in the chapter, however, the statistical analysis showed that, when other relevant background characteristics were controlled, Newport News residents were less likely to be very satisfied with their homes than were voucher recipients in the other three cities.

22. As a measure of the development's inadequacy, only one elevator served the three buildings.

23. Originally, 43 residents had received vouchers, but 8 recipients were later evicted or were dropped from the program for a variety of reasons.

24. Republic Management had a continuing contract with HUD's San Francisco office to manage HUD's foreclosed properties. It was serving in this capacity at Geneva Towers at the time of the vouchering out.

25. One key informant stated that the market did not affect the vouchering process as much as it would have under more typical market conditions. He indicated that the usual pattern in San Francisco was to lose many low-income families in situations like this because they could not afford to live in San Francisco without assistance. This problem was made worse by the fact that San Francisco has vacancy decontrols, meaning that every time a unit turned over, the rent was increased significantly, pushing more low-income families out of the city.

26. The findings discussed in this section are based on all families displaced in the vouchering out whose addresses could be geocoded, or 727 out of a total of 798 families.

27. Our results are broadly similar to those obtained by Goetz (2003) in his case study of the Hollman desegregation litigation in Minneapolis. Most of those displaced from public housing stayed in Minneapolis. More than half wound up on the north side of the city, and nearly three-fifths moved to a house within three miles of the original site.

28. Roughly 40 of the families relocated to the Reservoir Hill section of West Baltimore; one-half of these relocated to Renaissance Plaza, a collection of three high-rise apartment buildings—Temple Gardens, the Emersonian, and the Esplanade—located eight blocks north of Eutaw Gardens. The relocation of families on high floors at Renaissance created problems (e.g., children loitering in the

stairwells and in the hallways). The Renaissance example illustrates the fact that when vouchering out occurs, many voucher recipients may recluster in other multifamily properties (either high- or low-rise).

29. For a more detailed description of housing and neighborhood conditions in the more popular destination neighborhoods, interested readers are referred to the HUD report on the vouchering-out study (Varady and Walker 1998).

30. Popkin and Cunningham (2000) note that many Chicago Housing Authority tenants resisted relocation from dangerous developments because they were suspicious of the motivations for demolition. Some believed that the demolitions were being carried out to gentrify the area.

31. We relied on respondents' definitions of neighborhood boundaries; i.e., we did not define the terms "same neighborhood" or "nearby neighborhoods." It would have been useful to know, for example, when a Eutaw Gardens respondent said that she looked exclusively within the same Eutaw Gardens neighborhood whether she meant the Bolton Hill neighborhood of West Baltimore or West Baltimore as a whole. It was not practicable as part of this research project to determine whether respondents defined neighborhoods the same way or whether residents' perceptions of neighborhood boundaries coincided with the statistical neighborhoods used by city departments.

32. Respondents were asked: "When you were looking for a place to live after having to leave [NAME OF PROPERTY], did you feel that your welfare status, employment status, use of Section 8 voucher, race, sex, nationality, family size, or any handicap affected how you were treated?" If the respondent said yes, she/he was asked: "What do you feel was the main reason you were treated differently?"

33. Our results are therefore broadly similar to those obtained by Popkin and Cunningham in their 2000 study of Chicago Housing Authority residents. Few searchers had experienced racial discrimination. However, many respondents said that there were neighborhoods that they would not consider because of the likelihood of experiencing racial discrimination. Although discrimination on the basis of Section 8 status is illegal in Chicago, respondents' comments indicated that this type of discrimination is relatively common.

34. It would be a mistake to rely entirely on reports of discrimination to measure the incidence of discrimination because some movers may be unwilling to admit they have been discriminated against. A more reliable approach—and the one that has been used by HUD—is to send black and white testers to rental units and to compare their experiences (Yinger 1998).

35. Payment standards set by HUD are used to calculate the amount of rental assistance that a family will receive.

36. Our findings parallel those obtained by Popkin and Cunningham for Chicago Housing Authority displacees. There, most participants relied on information from friends and family and listings in newspapers.

37. Our results are similar to those reported by HUD in its first national assessment of HUD housing (HUD 1999). In a pilot of the first national survey

of residents of public housing, 75 percent of residents responded that they were satisfied or very satisfied with their dwelling units, and 64 percent said they would recommend their public housing development to a friend or family member. The survey, in its pilot stage, was to be expanded to full implementation and used as a tool by HUD in monitoring the nation's public housing.

38. The Kansas City case study contradicts this broad generalization. Larger families that moved to single-family homes experienced poor conditions.

39. In HUD's assessment of public housing, almost 75 percent of respondents felt safe in their unit day or night, although this dropped to about 50 percent when respondents were asked if they felt safe outside their buildings at night (HUD 1999).

40. It should be noted that among those who experienced no change in employment status were people who had retired or were disabled before the move.

41. To determine what types of counseling services had the greatest impact on levels of satisfaction with the new home, we entered the four summated scales measuring utilization of different types of help, along with other background characteristics, into a regression analysis limited to those who had utilized one or more of these counseling services. Only one of the four types of services played a statistically significant role (i.e., help in understanding lease or rental agreements, help in dealing with landlord or neighborhood problems after move-in). Householders who took advantage of this type of help were more likely to be satisfied with the housing search and were also more likely to be satisfied with their new home.

42. The effect of awareness of relocation services on housing satisfaction was modest because it occurred indirectly. That is, those who were unaware of relocation counseling services were more likely to feel unsafe in their neighborhood. The feeling of insecurity contributed to housing dissatisfaction.

43. The reader should keep in mind, however, that of the four vouchered-out sites, San Francisco householders moved the farthest.

3

Using Housing Vouchers to Move to the Suburbs

The movement from urban centers into suburban areas by low-income families that receive regular housing vouchers has been almost nonexistent in most parts of the United States. When families receiving Section 8 vouchers or certificates choose to relocate, they usually move only a short distance and remain within the central city. Alameda County, California's, experience stands in sharp contrast to these national residential patterns.[1] In the 1990s, one family in ten receiving assistance from the three housing authorities in the urban part of Alameda County (i.e., Oakland or Berkeley) moved to the suburban portion of the county and remained there. (See figure 3.1, which shows Alameda County, its location in the San Francisco East Bay Area, and its principal cities.) The widening dispersion of Section 8 families is clearly depicted in figures 3.2 and 3.3: the concentration of dots (each dot representing one voucher recipient) is much denser in suburban Alameda County in the 1999 map than was true in 1994.

In the late 1990s, the Alameda County pattern was of great interest to housing policymakers who wanted to know why Alameda County's Section

Portions of this chapter are adapted from David P. Varady and Carole C. Walker, "Using Housing Vouchers to Move to the Suburbs: How Do Families Fare? *Housing Policy Debate* 14, 3: 347–382. © 2003 Fannie Mae Foundation, Washington, D.C. Used with permission.

Portions of this chapter are adapted from David P. Varady and Carole C. Walker, "Using Housing Vouchers to Move to the Suburbs: The Alameda County, California, Experience," *Urban Affairs Review* 39, 2: 143–180. © 2003 SAGE Publications. Reprinted by permission of SAGE Publications.

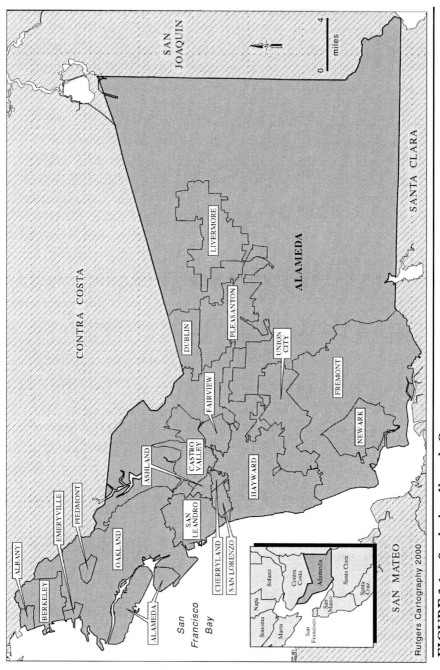

FIGURE 3.1 *Study site: Alameda County*

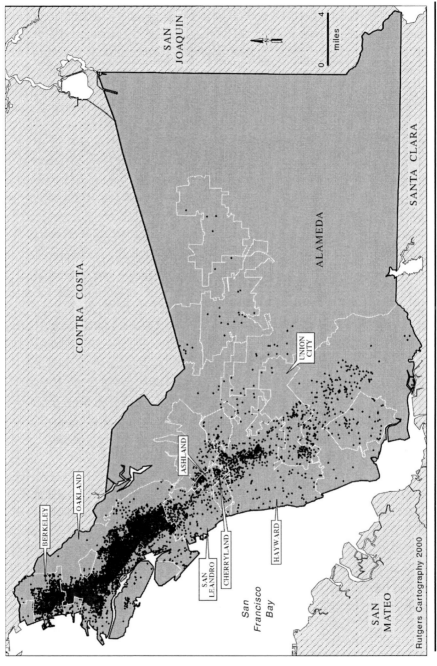

FIGURE 3.2   *Section 8 families: Overall distribution, 1994*

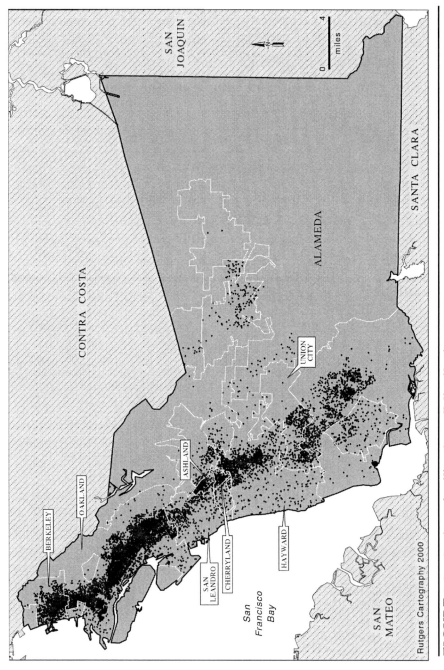

FIGURE 3.3   *Section 8 families: Overall distribution, 1999*

8 families had been able to suburbanize and whether this geographical shift had led to an improved quality of life.[2] Responding to this interest, the U.S. Department of Housing and Urban Development (HUD) contracted with the Center for Urban Policy Research at Rutgers University to carry out a case study in Alameda County addressing the following questions: What were the differences in housing search behavior between suburban movers (families that moved to the suburbs and remained there), local movers, and returnees (the families that moved to the suburbs and then returned to Oakland or Berkeley)? How did the families differ in the importance attached to the Section 8 briefing session? Did voucher recipients who moved to the suburbs encounter greater difficulties in searching for housing compared with families making local moves within Oakland or Berkeley? Were those moving to the suburbs less likely to be satisfied with their housing search because they were more likely to experience difficulties carrying it out, or were they more likely to be satisfied because they ultimately found better homes in nicer neighborhoods?[3] Did suburban movers become better off? Were the areas into which they moved more racially, ethnically, and socioeconomically diverse? Were suburban movers more likely to experience problems of adjustment at their new location? Were families that moved to the suburbs more likely than local movers and returnees to perceive improvements in their housing and neighborhood conditions when comparing their original and new locations? This chapter extends the analyses included in our 2000 HUD report (Varady and Walker 2000b).

On the basis of previous research (see chapter 1), we expected that suburban movers would experience more difficulty in carrying out their housing search and in adjusting to their new location. Conversely, the earlier research suggests that those who moved to the suburbs would be more likely to experience improvements in residential conditions, especially a greater sense of safety.

Our results refute the first hypothesis. Suburban movers were no more likely than those moving within Oakland or Berkeley to experience difficulties in carrying out their housing search, nor were they more likely to experience problems in adjusting to their new location. However, our findings did support the second hypothesis. Suburban movers were more likely than local movers to relocate to neighborhoods of higher socioeconomic status and were more likely to perceive improvements in neighborhood conditions between their new and old locations. Thus, Alameda County appears to be one place where voucher holders are able to move to the suburbs fairly easily.

Research Strategy

As in the vouchering-out study, a variety of data sources and methods were used in the Alameda case study. Data sources included a survey of voucher recipients; interviews with local housing officials, planning agency staff, rental agents, fair housing advocates, and others knowledgeable about housing issues in Alameda County; windshield surveys; HUD and housing authority documents; and a geographic information systems (GIS) analysis of neighborhood outcomes. Data were collected and analyzed to arrive at overall findings about the Section 8 voucher program in Alameda County.

The key source of data was a survey conducted in December 1999 of 300 householders who originally received housing vouchers from either the Oakland or the Berkeley housing authorities. The survey, which included open-ended as well as closed-ended questions, covered the housing search, the Section 8 briefing session, adjustment to the new location, current housing and neighborhood conditions (including safety), perceived changes between the original location and the current one, and objective housing and demographic characteristics.[4]

Because the focus of the study was on families that moved to the suburbs, a higher proportion of these families was interviewed.[5] Overall, 14 percent of the survey respondents were "nonmovers"—householders who remained in place when they received the Section 8 housing voucher; 32 percent were "local movers"—householders who moved from their original location after receiving the voucher, but who remained in Oakland or Berkeley; and 44 percent were "suburban movers"—householders who relocated from Oakland or Berkeley to the part of Alameda County under the jurisdiction of the Housing Authority of Alameda County and remained there. The remaining 10 percent were "returnees" who relocated to southern Alameda County but then moved back to Oakland or Berkeley.[6]

Most of those surveyed were black and female, and most were single parents. The average age of respondents was 48 years. The average income ($12,851) was low; 53 percent of respondents had incomes under $10,000. Twenty-one percent had not completed high school, 36 percent worked part or full time, and 24 percent received welfare assistance.

Suburban movers were significantly more likely to be younger (their average age was 43 years versus 61 for nonmovers and 50 for local movers) and were more likely to have children (68 vs. 55 percent for local movers and 32 percent for nonmovers). Suburban movers also had the highest average income level ($14,983 vs. $10,698 for local movers) and the highest proportion with a college education (19 vs. only 8 percent for nonmovers). The relatively high mean income for suburban movers may help to explain why they were able to cross the city/suburban boundary.

As part of the HUD study, we geocoded the addresses of the 300 survey respondents and were successful in matching 287 cases. We used the geocoded addresses to create a data file containing the respondent identification number, the distance moved (from the original location to the first voucher location, and from the original location to the location at the time of the 1999 survey), and four neighborhood socioeconomic characteristics of the census tract block group in which the household lived (median income, median house value, percentage black, and percentage Hispanic). Next, using the identification number as the common variable, we combined the geographic file and the survey file. The combined file was used for the analysis presented in this chapter.

The logistic regression component of the SPSS Inc. software package was used to test for the impact of different background characteristics on the respondents' satisfaction with their housing search and, in turn, on perceived changes in housing and neighborhood conditions. Table 3.1 lists the variables included in the logistic regression analysis and provides descriptive information on the sample of movers. Tables 3.2 and 3.3 present the logistic analysis results related to the determinants of satisfaction with the housing search; tables 3.4 and 3.5 present the findings related to the determinants of perceived changes in housing and neighborhood conditions, as well as changes in neighborhood safety.[7]

The Study Site

Located in the San Francisco East Bay Area, Alameda County is the seventh-largest county in California, encompassing a land area of more than 730 square miles. Its total population in 2000 was 1,443,741. The study site included the cities of Oakland and Berkeley and suburban Alameda County. For the purposes of the study, "suburban" Alameda

TABLE 3.1

Descriptive Information for Variables Included in the Regression Analysis

Variable	Definition	Local Mover	Suburban-Bound Mover	Returnee	All Movers	Significance
Background demographic characteristics						
Age	Age in years	49.8	43.11	42.93	45.58	****
Children under 18 in household	Dummy variable, where 1 = one or more children	54.6%	68.2%	63.3%	62.5%	
Married	Dummy variable, where 1 = married	5.2%	5.3%	13.3%	6.2%	
Black[a]	Dummy variable, where 1 = black	88.3%	82.4%	96.7%	86.3%	*
Employed at previous location	Dummy variable, where 1 = Employed	18.6%	21.5%	23.3%	20.6%	
Income	Household income from housing authority records in $000s	10.697	14.983	12.772	13.122	****
Education	Dummy variable, where 1 = attended college	8.3%	18.9%	3.3%	13.2%	**
Welfare at previous location	Dummy variable, where 1 = received welfare	58.3%	62.1%	60.0%	60.5%	
Gender	Dummy variable, where 1 = male	21.6%	5.3%	6.7%	11.6%	****
Background housing characteristics						
Housing density at original location	Dummy variable, where 1 = 0.75 persons per room or more	44.8%	48.1%	60.0%	48.2%	
Relocation counseling						
Briefing session very helpful	Dummy variable where 1 = briefing session very helpful	67.0%	59.8%	63.3%	62.9%	
Number of problems related to portability[b]	Dummy variable where 1 = one or more problems	NR	51.6%	65.5%	54.2%	
Housing search characteristics						
Days waited before started housing search	Dummy variable, where 1 = waited one week or more	40.0%	34.5%	28.6%	35.5%	
Days needed to find apartment	Dummy variable where 1 = 30 days or more	56.5%	66.7%	53.3%	61.5%	
Number of units looked at	Dummy variable where 1 = 4 or more places	45.9%	65.2%	73.3%	59.5%	***
Main source of information	Dummy variable, where 1 = friends or relatives	47.0%	24.4%	11.1%	30.9%	****
Looked at close neighborhoods only	Dummy variable, where 1 = original neighborhood and/or nearby neighborhoods	32.9%	12.9%	23.3%	21.1%	***
Looked at distant neighborhoods only	Dummy variable, where 1 = distant neighborhoods only, same city or rest of Alameda County	12.9%	27.3%	16.7%	21.1%	**

TABLE 3.1 (continued)

Variable	Definition	Local Mover	Suburban-Bound Mover	Returnee	All Movers	Signifi-cance
Had access to a car before the move	Dummy variable, where 1 = had access to car	49.5%	60.6%	70.0%	57.5%	*
Had access to a car at the time of the survey	Dummy variable, where 1 = had access to car	63.9%	75.8%	86.7%	72.6%	**
Preferred propor-tion of neigh-borhood resi-dents that should be like respondent	Dummy variable where 1 = half or more should be of same ethnic group, 0 includes those who said they didn't care or who refused to answer the question	26.8%	20.5%	20.0%	22.8%	
Discrimination encountered during the housing search	Dummy variable where 1 = encountered discrimination	22.9%	32.6%	40.0%	30.2%	
Difficulty in finding a home	Dummy variable, where 1 = experienced difficulty	48.2%	56.5%	55.2%	53.5%	
Satisfaction with the housing search	Dummy variable, where 1 = very satisfied	67.1%	59.2%	60.0%	62.0%	

Changes in residential conditions

Variable	Definition	Local Mover	Suburban-Bound Mover	Returnee	All Movers	Signifi-cance
More satisfied with current home	Dummy variable where 1 = more satisfied	67.5%	75.4%	50.0%	69.8%	*
More satisfied with current neigh-borhood	Dummy variable where 1 = more satisfied	56.6%	71.4%	42.9%	64.8%	*
Safer in current neighborhood	Dummy variable where 1 = safer	45.8%	68.7%	42.9%	58.0%	***
Current neigh-borhood more accessible	Dummy variable where 1 = more accessible (i.e., a score of 6 or more)	15.3%	49.6%	21.4%	34.6%	****
Current neighbor-hood better with regard to social environment	Dummy variable where 1 = better environment (i.e., score of 9 or higher)	44.7%	57.1%	57.1%	52.8%	
Current neighbor-hood worse with with regard to social and phys-ical problems	Dummy variable where 1 = worse environment (i.e., a score of 4 or higher)	49.4%	15.9%	64.3%	33.1%	****

[a] The "0" category includes whites, Asians, Hispanics (regardless of race), and people who said that they were "something else," those who answered "don't know," and those who refused to answer the question.

[b] Respondents were asked whether or not they had experienced any of the following problems in exercising portability: (1) the amount of paperwork, (2) the number of bedrooms allowed by the new authority, (3) having to provide the new housing authority with income and verifica-tion documents, (4) traveling around to find a unit, (5) different requirements set by the new and old housing authorities. An index was created by summing the number of problems cited.
* Significant at .10 level. ** Significant at .05 level. *** Significant at the .01 level. **** Signifi-cant at the .001 level.

TABLE 3.2

Logistic Regressions. Satisfaction with the Housing Search. Whether Very Satisfied with the Search. All Movers.[a]

	Logit Coefficients				
	(1)	(2)	(3)	(4)	(5)
Mobility characteristics					
Local mover (1 = local mover)[b]		.141	−.114	−.103	
Returnee (1 = returnee)[b]		−.197	−.246	−.276	
Housing search characteristics					
Briefing session (1 = very useful)		1.631****	1.601****	1.612****	1.681****
Housing search difficult (1 = search somewhat or very difficult)				−.697*	−1.051****
Constant	−.605	1.207	.386	.812	.188
−2 Log-Likelihood	266.834	240.030	229.810	226.712	237.597
Model chi-square	11.611	38.414****	48.634****	51.732****	40.847****
Improvement chi-square		26.803****	10.220****	3.098*	

Note: [a]This condensed table includes only statistical results for the mobility characteristics and the other significant predictors. The following variables proved to be statistically insignificant: age, children, married, black, employed at previous location, education, welfare status, gender, housing density, days waited before the housing search, days needed to find apartment, number of units looked at, main source of information for the housing search, discrimination, looked at close neighborhoods only, looked at distant neighborhoods only, access to auto, and preferred neighborhood ethnic composition. Results based on unweighted data ($N = 214$). Five separate computer runs were estimated: (1) demographic and housing characteristics only; (2) demographic and housing characteristics plus mobility characteristics; (3) demographic and housing characteristics, mobility characteristics, plus housing search characteristics; (4) demographic and housing characteristics, mobility characteristics, housing search characteristics, plus the perceived difficulty of the housing search; and (5) significant predictors of housing satisfaction. [b] Reference category = suburban movers.
*Significant at .10 level. ** Significant at .05 level. *** Significant at .01 level. ****Significant at .001 level.

County was defined as the part of the county under the jurisdiction of the Housing Authority of Alameda County. It did not include the far eastern, undeveloped portion. The major economic and geographic divide in the county is formed by the East Bay Hills, which run north to south. The hills, with their panoramic views of the San Francisco Bay Area, contain higher-income residential neighborhoods. The downtown sections and older, poorer neighborhoods are found in the flatland areas of the cities, where most of the population is concentrated.

TABLE 3.3

Logistic Regressions. Satisfaction with the Housing Search.
Whether Very Satisfied with the Search. Model Includes Number of
Portability Problems. Suburban Movers and Returnees Only.[a]

	Logit Coefficients				
	(1)	*(2)*	*(3)*	*(4)*	*(5)*
Demographic and mobility characteristics					
Age (years)	.050**	.040	.037	.034	
Welfare status (1 = received welfare at original location)	−.228	−.587	−1.388**	−1.590**	−.926**
Returnee (1 = returnee)[b]		−.078	−.238	−.247	
Housing search characteristics					
Briefing session (1 = very useful)		1.801****	1.580***	1.626***	1.678****
Portability problems (1 = one or more problems)[c]			−1.743****	−1.564***	−1.581****
Housing search difficult (1 = search somewhat or very difficult)				−.766	
Constant	−1.503	−2.439	.377	.826	.966
−2 Log-Likelihood	166.541	147.555	125.899	124.125	139.180
Model chi-square	14.395	33.380****	55.036****	56.811****	41.756****
Improvement chi-square		18.985****	21.656**	1.755	

Note: [a]This condensed table includes only statistical results for the mobility characteristics and the other significant predictors. The following variables proved to be statistically insignificant: children, married, black, employed at previous location, education, gender, housing density, days waited before the housing search, days needed to find apartment, number of units looked at, main source of information for the housing search, discrimination, looked at close neighborhoods only, looked at distant neighborhoods only, access to auto, and preferred neighborhood ethnic composition.
Results based on unweighted data (N = 162). Five separate computer runs were estimated: (1) demographic/housing characteristics only; (2) demographic/housing characteristics plus mobility characteristics; (3) demographic/housing characteristics, mobility characteristics, plus housing search characteristics; (4) demographic/housing characteristics, mobility characteristics, housing search characteristics, plus the perceived difficulty of the housing search; and (5) significant predictors of satisfaction with the housing search.
[b] Reference category = suburban movers
[c] Respondents who exercised portability were asked whether each of the following features constituted a problem: (1) the amount of paperwork; (2) the number of bedrooms allowed by the new housing authority; (3) having to provide the new housing authority with income and verification documents; (4) traveling around to find a unit; and (5) different requirements for clients set by the new and the old housing authorities. A scale was created by summing the number of problems experienced by the respondent; scale scores ranged between 0 and 5. The scale was recoded into two groups: (1) those who had experienced no problems, and (2) those who had experienced one or more problems.
* Significant at the .10 level. ** Significant at the .05 level. *** Significant at the .01 level.
**** Significant at the .001 level.

TABLE 3.4

Logistic Regressions. Impacts of Demographic Characteristics and
Mobility Status on Perceived Changes in Housing Conditions,
Neighborhood Conditions, and Crime.

Characteristic	Current Home Is Better	Current Neighbor- hood Is Better	Crime in Current Neighborhood Is Worse
Demographic characteristics			
Age (years)	.039**	.013	−.027
Children (1 = 1 or more)	.431	−.551	1.255*
Married (1 = married)	7.794	.551	−7.360
Black (1 = black)	-.600	−.759	.848
Employed (1 = employed)	.440	.350	−.221
Household income ($1,000)	−.031	.031	−.022
Education (1 = completed some college)	.111	−.348	−.309
Welfare status (1 = receive welfare)	.653	.244	−.664
Mobility status[a]			
Local mover (1 = local mover)	−.678*	−.577*	1.209**
Returnee (1 = returnee)	−1.444***	−.598	2.283****
Constant	−.318	.727	−2.632*
−2 Log-Likelihood	264.038	292.730	149.472
Model chi-square	31.748****	16.312*	39.954****

Note: Results based on unweighted data, N = 259.
[a] Reference category = suburban-bound movers.
*$p < .1$, **$p < .05$, ***$p < .01$, ****$p < .001$

During the 1990s, Berkeley and Oakland were experiencing the tightening housing market and price increases that had occurred earlier in other
parts of the Bay Area. The availability of affordable rental housing in the
inner suburbs (e.g., Hayward, San Leandro) enabled many to fulfill their
moving wishes.[8]

Neighborhoods of Origin

An analysis of the records of Section 8 clients in Oakland and Berkeley
from 1976 to 1999 showed that almost all the families moving to suburban Alameda County (91 percent) came from Oakland.[9] Oakland is the
largest and most densely populated city in the county. With its much
smaller client base, Berkeley was the origin of only 9 percent of the fami-

TABLE 3.5

Logistic Regressions. Impacts of Demographic Characteristics and Mobility Status on Indices Measuring Changes in Neighborhood Social and Physical Conditions, Accessibility, and the Quality of the Social Environment.

Characteristic	Worse Social and Physical Conditions	Better Accessibility	Better Social Environment
Demographic characteristics			
Age (years)	−.010	−.001	.015
Children (1 = 1 or more)	.188	−.182	−.062
Married (1 = married)	−.699	1.186*	−.562
Black (1 = black)	.405	.632	−.550
Employed (1 = employed)	.592	−.448	.310
Household income ($1,000)	−.002	.012	−.016
Education (1 = completed some college)	−.043	.467	.540
Welfare status (1 = receive welfare)	−.178	.270	.003
Mobility status[a]			
Local mover (1 = local mover)	1.845****	−1.698****	−.480
Returnee (1 = returnee)	2.399****	−1.468****	.154
Constant	−1.949	−.561	.184
−2 Log-Likelihood	249.583	272.741	318.829
Model chi-square	48.565****	37.169****	11.285

Note: Results based on unweighted data, *N* = 259.
[a] Reference category = suburban-bound movers.
*p < .1, **p < .05, ***p < .01, ****p < .001

lies moving to the suburbs. Both cities are racially and ethnically diverse. Oakland (total population, 399,484 in 2000) was 77 percent minority in 2000—up from 68 percent in 1990. Berkeley (total population 102,743 in 2000) was 45 percent minority in 2000.

Distressed socioeconomic conditions characterized both cities in the 1990s, particularly Oakland. Its poverty rate, 19 percent in 1990, was the highest in Alameda County (U.S. Bureau of the Census 1990). Berkeley's poverty rate was nearly 18 percent, the second highest rate in the county. Although the number of crimes reported in Oakland steadily decreased during the 1990s, crime statistics still were disturbing. In 1998, reported crimes in Oakland accounted for a disproportionate 48 percent of all crimes in the county—Oakland's population was about 29 percent of the total population of the county (State of California, Office of the Attorney General, Criminal Justice Statistics Center 2000). Oakland's public schools also had problems. According to the State of California's Department of Education (2000) statistics for the 1999–2000 school year, approximately 24 percent of the city's students dropped out of school and only about 25 percent of the students scored at or above the 50th percentile in reading and mathematics. By contrast, Berkeley's schools had a record of achievement, with statistics that surpassed both those of the county as a whole and those for the suburban communities to which Berkeley's Section 8 residents moved. In most Berkeley schools, for the 1999–2000 school year, more than half of the students scored above the 50th percentile in reading and mathematics.

Most Section 8 families in Oakland and Berkeley moving to the suburbs came from neighborhoods in the flatlands. Oakland's suburban movers primarily came from Elmhurst, Central East Oakland, San Antonio, and Fruitvale (see figure 3.4).[10] Nearly all of Berkeley's suburban-bound families came from South Berkeley, West Berkeley, and Central Berkeley. In general, these are distressed neighborhoods that the city had targeted for redevelopment (see Barton 1999; City of Oakland 1998).

Destination Neighborhoods

Three communities were the primary destinations of most of the Section 8 families that migrated into suburban Alameda County: Hayward, San Leandro, and Ashland (the destinations of 32, 26, and 11 percent of the movers, respectively). Smaller numbers of families moved to Fremont, Union City, Cherryland, and San Lorenzo. These communities varied considerably in socioeconomic characteristics, urban form, and governance, but in general, they were more affluent and they had lower proportions of minorities, higher household incomes, and lower poverty rates than Oakland and Berkeley.

During the 1990s, this part of the county was experiencing the greatest population growth and housing construction activity. Less-expensive housing was available in these communities, and the housing stock was newer and more typically suburban than the housing stock in Berkeley and Oakland. Commercial strips and shopping centers generally were well maintained and had more product variety than the convenience stores that served lower-income neighborhoods in Berkeley and Oakland. The Bay

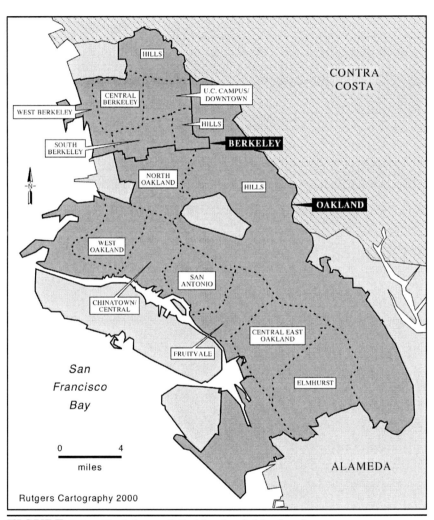

FIGURE 3.4 *Berkeley and Oakland neighborhoods*

Area Rapid Transit (BART) system extended into San Leandro, Hayward, Union City, and beyond, providing access to the entire Bay Area. Like many inner suburbs in the United States, however, some sections of some of the suburban communities were confronting increasing amounts of the crime, drug dealing, and juvenile delinquency associated with central cities.

Hayward and San Leandro had their own school districts; the San Lorenzo district covered Ashland and part of Cherryland. The student population was largely minority, and statistics on educational achievement indicated achievement levels that were better than those for Oakland (but lower than those for Berkeley). Compared with students in Oakland, more students in the suburban school districts scored at or above the 50th percentile in reading and mathematics; the average SAT scores for suburban high school seniors were also higher. A major difference, said a resident active in local affairs, was that the suburban schools did not have the problem of gangs—a problem that existed in Oakland.

Housing Authorities

Three housing authorities provided housing assistance in the case study area: the Berkeley Housing Authority (BHA), the Oakland Housing Authority (OHA), and the Housing Authority of Alameda County (HACA). BHA's and OHA's jurisdictions encompassed the cities they served; HACA's jurisdiction covered most of the smaller cities and suburban parts of the county, including the cities of Albany, Dublin, Emeryville, Fremont, Hayward, Newark, Pleasanton, and San Leandro; the unincorporated cities of Castro Valley and San Lorenzo; and the unincorporated areas of Ashland and Cherryland.[11] In the late 1990s, OHA's Section 8 voucher program provided assistance to approximately 9,600 families, HACA's program provided assistance to approximately 4,500 families, and BHA's program provided assistance to 1,450 families.

Portability and Section 8 Counseling in Alameda County

The families that moved from Oakland and Berkeley to suburban Alameda County took advantage of *portability*—a feature of the Section 8 program that permits voucher recipients to move from the issuing housing authority's jurisdiction into the jurisdiction of another authority. Families moved from the jurisdiction of the Oakland and Berkeley housing authorities (the authorities issuing the voucher) into the jurisdiction of the HACA. Among the factors facilitating portability in Alameda was the spirit of cooperation that developed between the housing authorities in Alameda County and their commitment to implementing the program.[12] The executive director of the Alameda County Housing Authority, which is considered one of the best-managed and innovative authorities in the nation, played a leadership role in this regard.[13]

By the mid-1990s, the executive directors and middle-level staff communicated regularly with each other and worked on resolving conflicts. Together, they adopted formal and informal administrative procedures that made it easier for clients to relocate to the Alameda suburbs. In the late 1990s, all three authorities began absorbing incoming Section 8 families from other jurisdictions, which eased many of the administrative and financial burdens associated with implementing portability.[14] HUD's San Francisco office also supported the housing authorities in administering the Section 8 voucher program and thus helped make the program work.

External factors, as well as program planning and operations, probably played a role in the higher incidence of suburbanization in Alameda County. Local housing experts and others interviewed for the study speculated that there may be greater acceptance of racial and ethnic diversity in the East Bay Area than there is elsewhere in the United States.[15] In addition, they said, neighborhood attachments tend to be weaker in Western cities than in the cities of the East and the Midwest. The boundary between city and suburbs is also less psychologically distinct in the West. Section 8 families in Oakland and Berkeley were probably less influenced by jurisdictional boundaries when they searched for a new home than families in other parts of the country (Davis 1998; Wiest 1998).[16]

Searching for Housing

Before conducting the study, we had assumed that suburban movers would have conducted the most extensive searches and encountered the most difficulty carrying out the search. As we shall see, this hypothesis was not supported.

Motivations for Moving

One might have expected that the families that moved to the suburbs would be more likely than local movers to be motivated by a desire for better neighborhood conditions; however, there were insignificant differences between the groups in the reasons given for moving from their original location. When asked to state the "most important reason" for moving, about half of all of the respondents (52 percent) cited unsatisfactory housing arrangements—some had outgrown their space; others were living with family members. For those living with their families, the housing voucher had given them the opportunity to become independent. A respondent who moved to Hayward said, "I was 27 years old with two kids living with my mother, and I needed a place of my own."

Nearly one-fifth wanted to get away from neighborhood problems: crime or drug dealing (11 percent) or other problems (7 percent). Two respondents mentioned that they had been raped, and many complained that their old neighborhood was unsafe, with drug dealing, robberies, assaults, and the sound of gunshots every night. "When I got my certificate," said one, "I was very happy because it was so bad where I was living; I was afraid for my children." A small group of respondents (8 percent) moved because they were displaced (e.g., their landlord stopped accepting Section 8 vouchers or a new landlord would not accept them); 7 percent said that they had to move because the rent became too expensive ("I had to move because they upgraded the apartment; they also upgraded the rent"); and 11 percent said that with housing assistance from Section 8, they could now afford to move and to a better and safer place. Said one, who moved from Oakland to San Leandro,

> [I moved] for a better area. In West Oakland there were a lot of shootings and drugs. I needed a safer environment for me and my kids. . . . I wanted to live in a neighborhood where my kids and I could walk to the store and there would be no shootings in broad daylight and no young people hanging out at the corner stores. We have a neighborhood watch in this neighborhood.

A final group (4 percent) said that they had personal reasons (e.g., they wanted to make a fresh start—they had gotten off drugs or wanted to escape an abusive relationship).

Beginning the Search, Time Spent Looking, and Number of Units Considered

A priori, it might be assumed that families moving to the suburbs would start looking for housing earlier, spend more time looking, and look at more units. Only the third hypothesis was supported. Suburban movers and returnees were significantly more likely than local movers to look at four or more places (see table 3.1). It is unclear why returnees more closely resembled suburban-bound than local movers with respect to this aspect of the housing search. However, it is possible that many of the returnees first looked unsuccessfully in the suburbs before settling on a place back in Berkeley or Oakland. If this was the case, returnees may have had to look at more housing units.

Families that moved to the suburbs and remained there fell in the middle of the three groups of movers on these measures. Nearly two-thirds (66 percent) began looking within one day of receiving their voucher, one-fifth (19 percent) started their search within a week, and fewer than one-fifth (15 percent) waited more than a week—beginning their search slightly more quickly than returnees, but more slowly than local movers. (On average, after receiving their voucher, families waited 13 days before starting the housing search.) Seventy-one percent of the suburban movers that remained in the suburbs were able to find a unit within two months, compared with 65 percent of those that later returned to Oakland or Berkeley. More than three-quarters of local movers found a unit within two months. Families moving to and remaining in the suburbs looked at 8 units; local movers looked at 4 units; and those that later moved back to Oakland or Berkeley looked at the most units (an average of 10). Overall, respondents looked at an average of about 7 housing units before deciding where to move.

Sources of Information

As we had anticipated, families moving to the suburbs relied more on newspaper listings for information used in the housing search, while local movers relied more on friends and relatives. Overall, the most frequently cited source of information used in the housing search was newspaper listings, mentioned by 39 percent of suburban movers; friends and relatives were mentioned by 24 percent. Three other sources also were mentioned: driving or walking around different locations (14 percent), housing

authority or other governmental professionals (13 percent), and real estate agents (10 percent).

Housing Relocation Services

Because families moving to the suburbs were more likely to be conducting their housing search in unfamiliar territory, it would seem reasonable
to assume that they would have been more dependent on information provided to them at the briefing session.[17] In fact, there were no significant
differences among members of the three mobility status groups with respect to assessing the usefulness of the briefing session; nor were there significant differences between members of the three subgroups in explaining
why the briefing sessions were helpful.

As with those in the two other respondent groups, nearly all suburban movers found the Section 8 voucher or certificate briefing session to
be helpful, and a majority found the session to be "very helpful" (60 percent).[18] When asked why the briefing session was helpful, respondents in
all three mobility groups cited similar reasons. The most helpful aspect of
the briefing, they said, was information about the Section 8 program, such
as how the program worked, its rules and regulations, how payments were
determined, the time frame for finding a unit to rent, and their rights and
obligations as tenants. Tips on what to look for in their housing search
were also appreciated. "They told us if we didn't have a car, [we should]
find a place that was convenient to things like buses, schools, and transportation," said one respondent. One remembered that she was warned during
the briefing session to watch out for hidden costs when looking for a unit:

> They gave me some insight on when a person gets into the apartment to
> make sure if you have to pay for water or electricity. Some apartments have
> electric heat. That would make your rent more expensive [and] that defeats
> the purpose of Section 8.

Others found the briefing session's information on how to present themselves and how to sell the program to a potential landlord useful.

Respondents were asked to specify additional services that might have
helped them when they first received their Section 8 voucher. Again, there
were no significant differences between the mobility groups, although some
services were mentioned by greater proportions of suburban movers than
by the others. The suggestion mentioned most frequently by suburban

movers (48 percent), as well as by those in the other mobility groups, was to provide better listings of housing vacancies that would include landlords or housing developments accepting Section 8 vouchers, cover a wider range of localities, and include listings of larger apartments. Respondents complained that the few listings that were provided were inaccurate or unsatisfactory. "The listing that they gave me didn't have much [from which] to choose. . . . It didn't [contain] areas where I wanted to live." Some respondents said that they were unfamiliar with the neighborhoods where some apartments were listed and wasted time looking at places that were in undesirable locations.

Families moving to the suburbs also wanted better information (16 percent) about the program and more financial assistance (16 percent), the latter probably because average rents were increasing so rapidly throughout the Bay Area. Providing additional client services (particularly help with transportation) was less of an issue for suburban movers than for local movers. Several respondents mentioned that they wished they had been told about the portability option at the briefing session—they had often found out about it later. Said one respondent who eventually did move to the suburbs, "I didn't know until after a while that I could move from city to city or anywhere in the country."

Finally, some personal attention would have been appreciated, especially by nonmovers and local movers: "Maybe a representative could have called to see how things were going to see if I needed assistance since my time was running out," said one. First-time renters were particularly lost: "There should have been a housing counselor to help people who are doing this for the first time, or a workshop," suggested one. Respondents in all three mobility groups suggested ways the briefing sessions could be improved, but those who moved to the suburbs and remained there were more likely to express their satisfaction with the briefing session than members of the other mobility groups. Said a 40-year-old mother of two who moved from Oakland to Hayward, "I was completely satisfied with the overall service they provided me and my family. Without them, I do not know what I would have done."

Geographic Scope of the Search

As expected, families moving to the suburbs were significantly more likely to limit their housing search to only distant neighborhoods or to sites outside the original city. Twenty-seven percent of suburban movers looked for housing only in distant neighborhoods within the original city; 17 percent limited their search to neighborhoods outside their original city. Conversely, local movers were more likely than suburban movers to limit their housing search to their original neighborhood or to nearby neighborhoods (see table 3.1).

Neighborhood Attributes Sought in the Housing Search

There was no support for the notion that in their housing search, families that moved to the suburbs and remained there would place more of an emphasis on neighborhood characteristics, such as safety and good schools, whereas local movers would stress their familiarity with the area. When asked why they had they had chosen to search for housing in a particular neighborhood, 45 percent of suburban movers said that the area was "familiar" or that they had always wanted to live there. "I wanted to be somewhere where there was opportunity," said one. "I always wanted to move to San Leandro, and I do all my business out here," said another.

Others who moved to the suburbs emphasized the following factors: 15 percent were attracted by a neighborhood's convenience ("the neighborhood I was looking at was close to buses and BART"), 14 percent sought better schools ("I wanted my kids to go to a Hayward school; I didn't want them to go to an Oakland public school—I figured that they would get a better education in the Hayward School District"), 10 percent looked in areas where friends or relatives resided, and 7 percent said that they were looking for a safer neighborhood ("I just wanted to get out of Oakland where there were shootings and everything. I just got far away from Oakland").

Many suburban movers were looking for specific neighborhood features. One said that she had looked for an area with "job opportunities, better housing, and better education for my children," adding that "basically I am trying to raise my children from the inner-city neighborhoods." Another said, "I wanted to stay in the area between San Leandro and Oakland. I looked for places that had public transportation close by, a clean environment with no drugs, no people hanging out; just quiet and peaceful." For 10 percent, however, Section 8 restrictions impinged on their search, some taking a unit because their time limit was about to run out and others settling for a place because of the reluctance of landlords to rent to voucher holders.

Neighborhood Ethnic or Racial Preferences

Although it might be assumed that suburban movers and returnees would place less emphasis on living in racially and ethnically homogeneous neighborhoods than would local movers, we found that this was not the case. In fact, Alameda County respondents as a whole tended to be indifferent to neighborhood racial and ethnic composition, or, if they cared at all, they preferred mixed over homogeneous neighborhoods, which may have contributed to the comfort level of movement in and out of communities in the area.

All respondents, nonmovers as well as movers, were asked, "Thinking about what you would prefer in terms of the neighborhood you live in, . . . what percentage of your neighbors would you prefer to also be [phrase inserted to match the respondent's race/ethnicity]?" Responses were coded into 10 categories ranging from all of them/100 percent to fewer than 10 percent. Differences in ethnic/racial preferences were not statistically significant between the three mover groups. Almost half the 300 survey respondents (46 percent) said that they did not care about the neighborhood's racial or ethnic composition. Another 10 percent did not know or would not answer the question. The remaining 132 respondents expressed the following preferences: 50 percent preferred a neighborhood where fewer than half their neighbors shared their race or ethnic background, 35 percent preferred a neighborhood that was "half and half," and 15 percent preferred a neighborhood where members of their race or ethnic group were in the large majority (two-thirds or more).[19]

Discrimination

In contrast to expectations, suburban movers were not significantly more likely to experience discrimination than were local movers. More than two-thirds of the respondents moving into suburban Alameda County said that they had not experienced discrimination in their housing search. Among respondents who reported discrimination, most (62 percent) said that it was because of their Section 8 status. (There were no significant differences in this statistic by mobility group.) Respondents reported either that landlords simply refused to accept tenants with vouchers or that they believed landlords held negative stereotypes about voucher holders—for example, that Section 8 tenants damaged property, were not employed, or were unreliable about paying rent. One respondent who moved to the suburbs described her experiences trying to rent a place:

> They think that they are too good for us people who have vouchers. . . . One owner did not want to show me the place. I asked if I could see it anyway. He said, "What for? You can't afford it." That's a turnoff—you're like, "Excuse me?" I feel like even though I have a voucher that I'm the same. Just because I have a Section 8 voucher doesn't make me less of a human being.

The tight housing market that a higher proportion of suburban movers cited as the most difficult aspect of their housing search may have enabled landlords to be more selective in choosing renters and to seek non–Section 8 tenants. The second most frequently mentioned type of discrimination—racial discrimination—was mentioned by one-sixth (17 percent) of those who said that they had experienced discrimination.[20] Other, less frequently cited, reasons for being discriminated against included presence of children (7 percent), physical appearance (5 percent), youth (5 percent), bad credit history (2 percent), and the fact that the landlord simply said "no more vacancies" (2 percent).

Automobile Access

It was reasonable to assume that families moving to the suburbs, whose housing searches covered a larger geographical area, might have had more access to a car than other respondents did. The survey did show that there were significant patterns by mover group. However, returnees, rather than families remaining in the suburbs, were the ones most likely to have access to a car at both the time of receipt of a Section 8 housing voucher and at the time of the survey. There is no obvious reason why those moving back to Oakland or Berkeley were more likely to have access to a car than movers who remained in the suburbs. As expected, local movers were least likely to have access at both points.

Three-fifths of the respondents moving to suburban Alameda County (61 percent) said that they had access to a car when they received their Section 8 voucher—the percentage rose to 76 percent at the time of the survey. Fifty-two percent had access to a car both when they received the Section 8 voucher and at the time of the survey, 15 percent lacked access at both times, 9 percent had shifted from having access to having no access, and 24 percent shifted from having no access to having access.[21]

Although it might be expected that access to a car would enable families to start their search sooner, spend less time on it, visit more units, rely more on "driving around" as an information source, and examine distant sites, this was not the case. Instead, on average, families with access to a car waited longer than those without access to start the search (about 18 days compared with 6 days) and spent more time on the search (44 days compared with 33 days). The differences, however, were not statistically significant.

Problems with Using Portability

Families moving to the suburbs were asked if they had experienced any of five specific problems associated with using portability. Of the five problems listed, by far the most frequently mentioned was difficulty in traveling around to look at units (42 percent).[22] Other problems for respondents moving to the suburbs, in order of their frequency, were (1) the authorization of fewer bedrooms by the new housing authority than were allowed in the respondent's previous jurisdiction (16 percent), (2) difficulties caused by varying requirements between the housing authorities (14 percent), (3) excessive paperwork required by the Section 8 program (11 percent), and (4) income verification (11 percent). A scale was created by summing the number of portability problems experienced by the respondent. Forty-six percent experienced no problems, 30 percent experienced one problem, whereas the remaining 24 percent experienced two or more problems. Returnees were somewhat but not significantly more likely to experience one or more problems than those moving to and remaining in the suburbs.

Difficulties in the Housing Search

Despite the small numbers of Section 8 voucher recipients at the national level making city-to-suburban moves, and despite media reports of resistance by suburbanites to voucher recipients, the families that moved to the suburbs that were surveyed for this study were not significantly more likely than local movers to report difficulties in the housing search. Proportionally, however, a greater share of the suburban movers than local movers did say that their search for housing had been difficult: 57 percent of suburban movers compared with 48 percent of local movers. The most common problem among respondents who experienced difficulty was the tightness of the housing market (mentioned by 71 percent of the suburban movers and 58 percent of local movers), followed by problems with child care or transportation.[23]

Although the differences in the types of problems faced by the three groups were not statistically significant, it is worth noting that a far higher proportion of returnees, compared with local movers or movers remaining in the suburbs, cited transportation problems or the lack of day care. For some returnees, these factors contributed to their decision to return from suburban Alameda County to Oakland or Berkeley. When asked how they overcame the difficulties reported in the housing search, there were no significant differences by subgroup in the techniques used. Like other types of movers, families moving to the suburbs said that they had found housing because of their own persistence (59 percent). They kept looking, exploring possibilities, and asking until they found a suitable, affordable apartment. Said a 48-year-old mother who moved from Oakland to San Leandro with her son,

> People would stereotype people with Section 8. They wouldn't rent [to me] because I had Section 8. I ignored it and just kept looking. You're always going to find someone who is different. It didn't really bother me, but I kept looking because I needed to find a place.

The other 41 percent highlighted a housing search technique. For example, a friend or relative would drive the respondent to various housing units, or the respondent would make a special effort to make a good impression on landlords. "I had to convince the landlord," said one successful searcher, the mother of two young children who moved to San Leandro, "that even though I was young, I was a responsible young lady. So I had to talk my way into an apartment."

Overall Satisfaction with the Housing Search

A priori, it was impossible to predict whether families moving to the suburbs would be more, or less, satisfied with their housing search than local movers. If suburban movers experienced a more difficult housing search (which we found in the preceding section was not the case), then they might be more dissatisfied with the search. Conversely, if they were happy with their new living situation, they might be satisfied with their search because of the good results. In reality, there were insignificant differences among local movers, suburban movers who stayed in the suburbs, and suburban movers who later returned to Oakland or Berkeley in the level of satisfaction with the process of searching for housing. A large majority of the respondents who moved to suburban Alameda and stayed there said that they had been satisfied with the housing search; 59 percent had been "very satisfied." This was, however, a smaller proportion than among local movers (67 percent) or returnees (60 percent).[24]

When dissatisfied respondents were asked to state their main reason for being unhappy with their housing search, by far the most frequently mentioned reason was inadequate housing assistance (63 percent), a response that included both a limited choice of housing and not enough help in finding housing. "There are not a lot of choices to choose from. You may have to move into a bad or a not very nice neighborhood just to get somewhere to live. Otherwise, you will lose your voucher," said a 39-year-old mother of three who moved from Oakland to Castro Valley. One respondent who moved to a substandard location laid the blame on previous Section 8 recipients:

> Here is something that you waited years for, and when you get it, the people have made the program so bad that you can't get find a decent place to live. The places you find are where gang-bangers and drug dealers hang out.

Other reasons respondents were unhappy with the housing search included the poor quality of available housing (22 percent), the deadlines imposed for finding a home (11 percent), and the substandard quality of the neighborhoods where housing was available (4 percent). There were insignificant differences by mobility group in responses to a question on the main reason for being dissatisfied with the search.

How Respondents Explained the Moves That They Made

Most of this chapter focuses on the impact of mobility status (i.e., whether the respondent was a suburban mover, a local mover, or a returnee) on perceived changes in residential conditions. However, another aim of our research was to look at householders' explanations for the type of move they made.

Why Did Some Voucher Recipients Move to the Suburbs?

Voucher recipients who moved into suburban areas of the county cited a variety of motivations, mentioning both negative aspects of their original locations ("push" factors) and positive aspects of their destination ("pull" factors). One-quarter of the families that moved into the suburbs cited problems in their original neighborhood as the reason for leaving. Drugs, crime, and noise had been common problems. Typical were the comments by one respondent: "The place where I lived, the neighbors sold drugs, there were shootings, and my car [was] stolen two times. The neighborhood was not too good." Another former Oakland resident who moved to Hayward mentioned that along with the bullet slugs she had found on her carpet, drug dealing in the neighborhood, and break-ins in the basement, someone had even stolen a turkey from her refrigerator. Respondents moved to the suburbs, they said, to escape the "ghetto" and to get themselves and their children out of a "drugged area." Some did so with the expressed intent of turning their lives around. "I moved to get out of Oakland," said a young mother who moved to Fremont. "I had old habits; I used to use drugs. I needed to get away from the people over there."[25] The Section 8 voucher and portability gave them the opportunity to escape their former neighborhood.

One-quarter of the respondents thought the suburbs would be a better place to live. They were attracted to the suburbs for many of the same reasons that middle-class families are, and they especially thought that the suburbs would be a better place to raise children. The suburbs were "family oriented," respondents said; they had "better schools," and they offered "a better life." As one mother said, "The places in Oakland that [accepted] Section 8 did not look good. Hayward has better-looking streets, and the area is better. Not too many people hang out on the streets, and the kids have more things to do out here. Also, the schools are better." Some suburban movers (approximately 14 percent) were familiar with the new area, often because other family members were living there.

One-quarter cited housing conditions as their reason for wanting to leave where they had been living. Included in this category were those who said that they wanted a better place to live (one with a washing machine and dryer, or one with a yard where the children could play) as well as those who said that they could not find affordable housing in their original neighborhood. Approximately 8 percent reported problems with their landlords where they had originally been living (e.g., the landlord did not maintain the premises, or a new owner did not accept housing vouchers). About 9 percent gave personal reasons for leaving their original location, such as a medical condition that necessitated a change (too many steps in their old place, or the need to be near their doctors) or a desire to change their lives. "I wanted to get a fresh start," said a respondent who moved to Hayward, "and I thought that move would be more productive for me." Only 3 percent mentioned that the Section 8 program facilitated cross-jurisdictional moves.

Why Did Some Voucher Recipients Choose Not to Move to the Suburbs?

Families that did not move to suburban Alameda County but remained where they were already living or moved within Oakland or Berkeley were asked why they had decided not to move to another town. Most frequently, respondents pointed to positive aspects of the neighborhood—more than half the respondents (56 percent) mentioned their nice neighbors, that they felt settled in, or the low incidence of crime where they were living as reasons for not moving to the suburbs. Respondents also cited convenience (where they lived was close to public transportation, stores, schools, family members, and churches, 18 percent); the location's advantages for raising children (e.g., they did not want to send the children to a new school, 10 percent); the difficulty of finding new housing with an affordable rent (10 percent); the problem of resistant landlords (e.g., landlords who would not accept Section 8 vouchers, 4 percent); or their unwillingness to leave a desirable house at the original location (1 percent). Only 2 percent of the respondents said that the time limits set by the program influenced their decision (families that could not find a place within the allotted time of 120 days risked losing their vouchers).

Why Did Some Families Move Back to Oakland or Berkeley after First Moving to the Suburbs?

Returnees were asked to provide the main reason for moving back to Berkeley or Oakland after using Section 8 assistance to relocate to suburban Alameda County. More than half cited positive aspects of the destination: 25 percent said that housing was cheaper or they had found a specific unit that they liked; 29 percent were attracted by neighborhood characteristics such as proximity to family; or because of other considerations such as greater accessibility to public transportation, stores, and jobs. Others cited negative aspects of the suburban locations as the main reason for moving back to Oakland or Berkeley. For example, 21 percent mentioned inconvenience, or problems with the neighborhood ("the apartment in San Leandro was [becoming like] the one in Oakland. [There was] drug trafficking, neighbors fighting, and kids hanging out all night"). Some 25 percent said that they had been unable to find affordable housing in the suburbs.

Why Did Some Families Not Move at All after They Received a Section 8 Voucher?

Three-fourths of the nonmovers said that they had not looked for another place to live, and when asked why they had not, three-fifths said that familiarity with their current neighborhood had made them want to stay where they were. "I have been here in Oakland all of my life. I just like Oakland. My family is close by," was a typical response among nonmovers. A smaller group of respondents cited convenience; satisfaction with their current housing; or personal factors, such as disabilities or old age, that prevented an active housing search as reasons for not wanting to search. Most of the respondents who had looked for a new home but had not moved cited the lack of affordable housing or the high cost of moving. A few mentioned that even though they had looked elsewhere, they had remained where they were living because of positive features of the location or disabilities that would make moving difficult.

Migration Patterns

The preceding section has shown that Oakland's and Berkeley's Section 8 families found it relatively easy to cross the city/suburban boundary. Furthermore, most were satisfied with the housing search. This raises the following questions: First, how far did families move once they crossed the city/suburban boundary? Second, what was the spatial distribution of the families before and after they received their vouchers? Third, to what types of neighborhoods did voucher recipients relocate?

Distance Moved

Survey respondents were asked to provide three addresses: the original address where they were living at the time they received their Section 8 voucher, the first address where they used their voucher, and their current address. Those who relocated when they first received their voucher moved an average of 5.1 miles (the distance between their first and second addresses). When comparing their original address with their current address (the first and third addresses), the average distance moved rose to 7.5 miles.

The average distances moved, however, obscure considerable variations among the three groups of movers. When they made their first move after receiving their voucher, suburban movers and returnees moved 6.8 miles and 5.2 miles, respectively; local movers moved just 3.6 miles. When the distances between their original address and their current address were calculated, those who moved to the suburbs and remained there were shown to have moved considerably farther than the other movers—an average 11.2 miles compared with 3.9 miles for returnees, and 3.5 for local movers.

As might be expected, those who focused their search only on distant locations were more likely to make long-distance moves, both in their first moves and to their current location. Specifically, more than three-fifths (63 percent) of those who considered distant neighborhoods only and no others moved five or more miles from their original to their current location, as compared with about half (49 percent) of those who did not limit their search in this way. In contrast to expectations, however, those who said that the Section 8 briefing session was useful were less likely to make long-distance moves (45 vs. 62 percent). Perhaps those who thought the sessions were not useful were already savvy about the housing market and, consequently, were already prepared to make long-distance searches and moves.

The Spatial Distribution of Families

At the time they received their Section 8 voucher, 82 percent of the surveyed families lived in Oakland and 17 percent lived in Berkeley. After their first move, the proportion of surveyed families living in Oakland decreased by 20 to 62 percent. The decrease in Berkeley was more modest—from 17 to 14 percent.

By the time of the survey in December 1999, the proportion of respondents living in Oakland had decreased even further, from 62 to 45 percent; the proportion living in Berkeley had declined only slightly, from 14 to 12 percent. Of the remaining respondents (43 percent), most were living in the jurisdiction of the HACA in three communities, Hayward, San Leandro, and Ashland, just to the south of Oakland. Nine percent were scattered among several other communities including Union City (4 percent), Emeryville (3 percent), and Castro Valley (2 percent).

Neighborhood Outcomes of the Move

In general, compared with local movers and returnees, suburban movers experienced greater socioeconomic improvement by moving into areas with more racial and ethnic diversity, higher incomes, and better housing values. Returnees made gains in their first move to the suburbs, but they then lost ground when they moved back to Oakland or Berkeley.

Table 3.6 compares the demographic and housing characteristics of the census tracts surrounding the suburban movers, local movers, and returnees at three locations: their original location at the time they first received the Section 8 voucher; their location after their first move; and their location at the time of the December 1999 telephone survey. This table also includes the socioeconomic characteristics of the census tracts surrounding nonmovers at all three points in time. Table 3.7 compares the members of the three mover groups in changes in these factors.

At the time that families received their Section 8 vouchers, the average suburban-bound recipient lived in a neighborhood where 58 percent of the residents were black. After receiving the voucher, the average suburban-bound family moved to a location where 35 percent of the residents were black; by the time of the telephone survey, the average family moving to suburban Alameda County lived in a neighborhood where just 13 percent of the residents were black—a notable change from the original location. Whereas suburban movers, on average, experienced a 45 percent decline in the proportion of blacks in their surrounding census tract, local movers, on average, experienced only a slight decrease (4 percent). Returnees experienced an 11 percent decrease in the proportion of blacks

TABLE 3.6

Comparison of Four Mover Groups by the Socioeconomic Characteristics of Their Census Tracts at the Time of Receipt of Voucher, after the First Move, and at the Time of the Telephone Survey

	Mobility Status					
			Suburban-		All	
		Local	Bound		Mobility	Signifi-
Characteristic	Nonmovers	Movers	Movers	Returnees	Groups	cance
Percentage black						
• At receipt of voucher	52.5%	54.0%	57.5%	54.6%	55.0%	
• After first move	52.5%	51.0%	35.2%	43.5%	43.5%	***
• At time of telephone survey	52.5%	49.8%	12.5%	60.3%	35.1%	***
Percentage Hispanic						
• At receipt of voucher	10.2%	15.9%	15.6%	14.8%	14.7%	*
• After first move	10.2%	14.9%	18.5%	18.0%	16.1%	***
• At time of telephone survey	10.2%	13.7%	19.7%	13.2%	15.8%	***
Median household income						
• At receipt of voucher	$22,606	$21,216	$23,708	$24,670	$22,827	
• After first move	$22,606	$23,217	$28,640	$28,442	$25,977	***
• At time of telephone survey	$22,606	$25,040	$32,961	$23,355	$27,980	***
Median house value						
• At receipt of voucher	$146,207	$130,620	$125,391	$132,626	$131,196	
• After first move	$146,207	$138,055	$155,287	$147,399	$147,068	
• At time of telephone survey	$146,207	$148,078	$179,476	$127,077	$159,296	***

*Significant at the .05 level. **Significant at the .01 level. ***Significant at the .001 level.
Source: U.S. Bureau of the Census, 1990.

after their move to the suburbs. When they returned to Oakland or Berkeley, however, their neighborhoods, on average, had higher concentrations of blacks than their original ones where they had been living at the time they received their vouchers (60 vs. 55 percent).

The patterns for the three mobility groups with respect to Hispanic composition are different from the patterns for racial composition. The figures indicate that Hispanics were more evenly distributed in the neighborhoods where voucher recipients lived at various points in time. Nevertheless, suburban movers experienced a significant increase in the proportion of Hispanics when they moved to their current neighborhood (from 16 percent in their original neighborhood to 20 percent in their current neighborhood). Local movers experienced a slight decrease in the pro-

TABLE 3.7

Changes between Original and Current Location in Demographic and
Housing Characteristics in the Surrounding Census Tract,
by Mover Group (*N* = 215)

Characteristic	Local Mover	Suburban- Bound Mover	Returnee	All Mobility Groups	Signif- icance
Change in percentage black	0.04	−0.45	0.06	−0.23	***
Change in percentage Hispanic	−0.02	0.04	−0.02	0.01	**
Change in median income level	$3,301	$9,552	−$1,315	$5,826	***
Change in median house value	$15,834	$54,858	−$5,549	$32,635	***

*Significant at the .05 level. **Significant at the .01 level. ***Significant at the .001 level.
Source: U.S. Bureau of the Census, 1990.

portion of Hispanic residents (from 16 percent in the original neighborhood to 14 percent in the current neighborhood).

Both suburban-bound and local movers experienced increases in median household income and in the median value of the houses in their
neighborhoods as a result of their moves. For families relocating to the
suburbs, the increases were significantly larger (39 percent for median
household income and 43 percent for median house value) than for local
movers (18 and 13 percent).

Returnees experienced increases in median household income and
in the median value of the houses in the neighborhood as a result when
they moved to the suburbs; however, when they moved back to Oakland
or Berkeley, they experienced decreases in both—18 percent in median
household income and 14 percent in median house value. In fact, returnees generally ended up worse off in terms of the median income and housing value of their neighborhoods at the time of the survey than they were
at the time they first received their vouchers (a drop of 5 percent in median income and 4 percent in housing value).

Thus, table 3.7 shows that at the time of the survey, those families
that had moved to the suburbs were significantly more likely than families that had made other types of moves to live in neighborhoods that were
less racially concentrated and had a higher median income and median
housing values than their original neighborhoods. They were also more
likely to live in neighborhoods that had higher concentrations of Hispanics than their original neighborhood.

Did Suburban Movers Experience Problems of Adjustment at Their New Location?

Previous research on housing mobility programs indicates that low-income renters experience adjustment problems when they move into middle-class suburban areas (Popkin, Galster, et al. 2000; Rubinowitz and Rosenbaum 2000). To learn whether suburban movers and returnees experienced more adjustment problems than local movers, the survey asked questions about respondents' relationships with landlords and neighbors and their children's adjustment in their new schools, both immediately after their move and six months later.

Suburban movers, local movers, and returnees did not differ significantly in their adjustment to their new locations. Regardless of their mobility status group, respondents reported few adjustment problems at the time of their move (see table 3.8). Eighty percent of the respondents said that their relationship with their neighbors immediately after the move was "good" or "excellent"; 83 percent reported that their relationship with their landlord was "good" or "excellent"; and 86 percent of the respondents who had children said that their adjustment to their new school was "good" or "excellent." There was remarkably little change in these indicators between the time of the move and six months later.

Tenants' Perspectives on Housing and Neighborhood Conditions

Previous research suggests that suburban movers would be more likely than local movers to achieve improved residential conditions and to move toward self-sufficiency. Our results generally supported the first, but not the second, hypothesis.

Changes in Housing and Neighborhood Conditions

Respondents were asked to compare their current home with the one where they were living at the time they received their housing voucher. As expected, suburban movers were more likely than local movers to believe that their current home was superior to their original one: 75 percent of the suburban-bound families and 68 percent of the local movers reported that they were more satisfied with their current home than their original one

TABLE 3.8

Adjustment to New Location: Differences between Local Movers,
Suburban Movers, and Returnees

| | Mobility Status | | | | |
Characteristic	Local Movers	Suburban-Bound Movers	Returnees	All Mobility Groups	Signif-icance
Relations with landlord immediately after move					
Excellent/good	84.3%	82.4%	85.2%	83.4%	N.S.
Fair/poor	15.7%	17.6%	14.8%	16.6%	
$N =$	83	131	27	241	
Relations with landlord six months after move					
Excellent/good	79.8%	78.6%	74.1%	78.5%	N.S.
Fair/poor	20.2%	21.4%	25.9%	21.5%	
$N =$	84	131	27	242	
Relations with neighbors immediately after move					
Excellent/good	81.9%	79.1%	78.6%	80.0%	N.S.
Fair/poor	18.1%	20.9%	21.4%	20.0%	
$N =$	83	129	28	240	
Relations with neighbors six months after move					
Excellent/good	83.1%	80.8%	78.6%	81.3%	N.S.
Fair/poor	16.9%	19.2%	21.4%	18.7%	
$N =$	83	130	28	241	
Adjustment of children to school immediately after move					
Excellent/good	87.9%	84.9%	90.0%	86.4%	N.S.
Fair/poor	12.1%	15.1%	10.0%	13.6%	
$N =$	58	106	20	184	

(see table 3.9). The biggest difference, however, was between suburban-bound and local movers on the one side, and returnees on the other. Only 50 percent of the returnees believed that their current home was superior.

Respondents who said that they were more satisfied with their current home were asked in an open-ended question why they felt that way (table 3.9). Although families in all three mover groups cited better housing conditions as the reason for reporting that they preferred their current to their original home, suburban movers were somewhat more likely

TABLE 3.8 (continued)

| | Mobility Status | | | | |
	Local Movers	Suburban-Bound Movers	Returnees	All Mobility Groups	Signif-icance
Characteristic					
Adjustment of children to school six months after move					
Excellent/good	87.9%	84.1%	90.0%	85.9%	N.S.
Fair/poor	12.1%	15.9%	10.0%	14.1%	
N =	58	107	20	185	
Change in relationship with landlord over first six months					
Excellent/good to excellent/good	78.3%	77.1%	74.1%	77.2%	N.S.
Excellent/good to fair/poor	6.0%	5.3%	11.1%	6.2%	
Fair/poor to excellent/good	1.2%	1.5%	0.0%	1.2%	
Fair/poor to fair/poor	14.5%	16.0%	14.8%	15.4%	
N =	83	131	27	241	
Change in relationship with neighbors over first six months					
Excellent/good to excellent/good	79.5%	77.5%	78.6%	78.3%	N.S.
Excellent/good to fair/poor	2.4%	1.6%	0.0%	1.7%	
Fair/poor to excellent/good	3.6%	3.1%	0.0%	2.9%	
Fair/poor to fair/poor	14.5%	17.8%	21.4%	17.1%	
N =	83	129	28	240	
Change in adjustment of children to school(s) over first six months					
Excellent/good to excellent/good	86.2%	82.1%	90.0%	84.2%	N.S.
Excellent/good to fair/poor	1.7%	2.8%	0.0%	2.2%	
Fair/poor to excellent/good	1.7%	1.9%	0.0%	1.6%	
Fair/poor to fair/poor	10.3%	13.2%	10.0%	12.0%	
N =	58	106	20	184	

Note: N.S. = not significant. Due to rounding, some of the columns do not add to 100 percent.

to emphasize a unit's modernity or better maintenance (local movers tended to emphasize the spaciousness of the unit). Typical comments by families that moved to the suburbs were "It's more updated and better quality"; "the other house was old"; "where I'm living now they fix up the place more"; and "it's cleaner." Some respondents singled out the laundry facilities—a plus for the suburban-bound families, which averaged more children than other types of movers. Other respondents emphasized superior neighborhoods as the main reason for preferring their new homes in the suburbs. Oakland, said one respondent, a 40-year-old mother of two, was "like the Bronx—gang- and drug-infested." By contrast, Hayward, she said, was "a nice, quiet area" with a "nice school for my children." Suburban movers appreciated the peace and safety of their new neighborhoods, particularly when compared with their old neighborhoods in Oakland. "There the neighborhood was bad—it was drugs sold on the corner. Here it's very quiet and secure," said a 48-year-old single woman who moved to Hayward from the Elmhurst section of Oakland.

Respondents were asked to compare their current neighborhood with the one where they had lived when they first received their voucher. The results were consistent with our expectations regarding the benefits of portability. Almost three-quarters of the suburban movers reported that they were more satisfied with their current neighborhood than with the one where they had lived before receiving a voucher; this was true for only about half the local movers and returnees. For those who were satisfied, there were insignificant differences in the reasons they gave in feeling this way. Nearly 60 percent reported that physical or social conditions were better in their new neighborhoods; suburban movers mentioned that the neighborhood was better for children (no returnees mentioned this reason); and more local movers cited the neighborhood's convenience as being better, but the differences in reasons were insignificant.

In their answers, suburban movers repeated and expanded on their earlier comments about their homes in explaining why they liked their current neighborhoods better—their current neighborhoods were "family-oriented," said one, with "a better class of people." "You don't hear guns going off, there are no liquor stores," said another. A single mother of one remarked that Oakland was "too ghetto. Here I can get peace of mind." One respondent, a 39-year-old mother of one, summarized for many the reasons that she preferred the suburban neighborhood, saying, "It is a very quiet neighborhood. Neighbors mind their own business, but everyone is very polite. Shopping and schools are near and very nice. I can sleep at night—there are no drugs, or guns, or people hanging out late at night; no break-ins to our homes."

Suburban movers were, as anticipated, more likely than other movers to perceive improvements in safety in their current neighborhood when compared with their original one. Nearly 70 percent of suburban movers felt safer at their current location, compared with 46 percent of local movers and 43 percent of returnees.

TABLE 3.9

Residential Satisfaction Indicators, by Mobility Status

	Mobility Status				
		Suburban-		All	
	Local	Bound		Mobility	Signif-
Characteristic	Movers	Movers	Returnees	Groups	icance
Current home compared with original one					
About as satisfied with current home, or more satisfied with previous home	32.5%	24.6%	50.0%	30.2%	*
More satisfied with current home	67.5%	75.4%	50.0%	69.8%	
N =	83	134	28	245	
Reason more satisfied with current home than with original one[a]					
Better housing conditions	72.2%	61.4%	76.9%	66.1%	N.S.
Better neighborhood conditions	24.1%	33.7%	23.1%	29.8%	
Convenience	3.7%	5.0%	0.0%	4.2%	
N =	54	101	13	168	
Reason less satisfied with current home than with original one[a]					
Worse neighborhood conditions	21.4%	16.7%	66.7%	28.1%	N.S.
Worse housing conditions	64.3%	83.3%	16.7%	62.5%	
Drugs or crime	14.3%	0.0%	16.7%	9.4%	
N =	14	12	6	32	
Current neighborhood compared with original one					
About as satisfied with current neighborhood, or more satisfied with original one	43.4%	28.6%	57.1%	35.2%	*
More satisfied with current neighborhood	56.6%	71.4%	42.9%	64.8%	
N =	83	133	28	244	
Reason more satisfied with current neighborhood[a]					
Better for children	4.3%	11.6%	0.0%	8.3%	N.S.
Convenience	14.9%	10.5%	6.7%	11.5%	
Better neighborhood conditions	59.6%	56.8%	73.3%	59.2%	
Less crime	21.3%	21.1%	20.0%	21.0%	
N =	47	95	15	157	
Reason less satisfied with current neighborhood[a]					
Worse neighborhood conditions	30.8%	42.9%	40.0%	36.0%	N.S.
Worse housing conditions	7.7%	14.3%	0.0%	8.0%	
Drugs or crime	61.5%	42.9%	60.0%	56.0%	
N =	13	7	5	25	
Safety of current neighborhood compared with original one					
Less safe or about as safe	54.2%	31.3%	57.1%	42.0%	***
Safer	45.8%	68.7%	42.9%	58.0%	
N =	83	134	28	245	

Note: N.S. = not significant. Due to rounding, some of the columns do not add to 100 percent.
[a] Results based on an open-ended question that was post-coded.
* Significant at the .05 level. ** Significant at the .01 level. *** Significant at the .001 level.

Respondents were asked to compare their current neighborhood with their original one with respect to 12 social and physical characteristics (table 3.10).[26] As one might expect, suburban movers were more likely than local movers or returnees to cite improvements in neighborhood conditions as a result of the move. A significant number singled out neighborhood schools, in particular, as better (74 percent of suburban movers compared with only 32 percent of returnees and 29 percent of local movers). A significant number of suburban residents also reported that people in their neighborhoods were more likely to have jobs compared with people in their old neighborhoods. Negative neighborhood characteristics, such as rundown houses, people using drugs, and people on welfare, were also significantly less likely in their suburban locations. Surprisingly, given the literature on the inconvenience of suburban locations, in Alameda this proved not to be a problem. In fact, a significant number of suburban respondents, compared with respondents living in Oakland or Berkeley, reported that their new neighborhoods offered more convenient shopping and better job opportunities. The only exception to this pattern was for people watching each other's children—more returnees mentioned this as a positive attribute of their new neighborhood compared with their original one.

Principal components analysis applied to the 12 neighborhood evaluations yielded a three-component solution (see table 3.11). The three components could be interpreted as the following factors: the extent to which the current neighborhood was (1) worse with respect to social and physical conditions, (2) better with respect to accessibility, and (3) better with respect to quality of the social environment. Summated scales were prepared for each of the three factors by adding up the number of positive/negative attributes. For example, the first scale (worse with respect to social problems) was based on six items. We added the four negative items and subtracted the two positive ones. Scale scores for this index originally ranged from −2 to 10. The scale was later recoded into two groups: (1) three or less, and (2) four or more.

As predicted, suburban-bound respondents scored lower on the index measuring the prevalence of social and physical problems at the current location. In other words, suburban movers were more likely to see their new neighborhoods as places where people had jobs, there were better schools, fewer people used drugs, there were fewer rundown houses, and there were fewer people on welfare. In terms of percentages, only 15

TABLE 3.10

Likelihood of Finding Specific Neighborhood Characteristics at Current
Location Compared with Original Location, by Mobility Status

		Mobility Status			
Characteristic	*Local Movers*	*Suburban-Bound Movers*	*Returnees*	*All Mobility Groups*	*Signif-icance*
Social and physical conditions					
People more likely to have jobs	34% (85)	62% (133)	29% (28)	48% (246)	***
Better schools	29% (85)	74% (134)	32% (28)	54% (247)	***
People use drugs	17% (85)	8% (133)	29% (28)	13% (246)	**
Rundown houses	17% (85)	6% (134)	29% (28)	12% (247)	***
People on welfare	15% (85)	8% (134)	25% (28)	13% (247)	*
Violent gangs	12% (85)	11% (133)	7% (28)	11% (246)	N.S.
Accessibility					
Convenient shopping	41% (85)	77% (134)	43% (28)	61% (247)	***
Better job opportunities	20% (85)	56% (133)	21% (28)	39% (246)	***
Social environment					
Neighborhood people know one another	28% (85)	33% (134)	32% (28)	31% (247)	N.S.
People help each other	28% (85)	44% (134)	39% (28)	38% (247)	N.S.
People watch children	32% (85)	49% (133)	54% (28)	44% (246)	*
See friends or relatives	28% (85)	29% (134)	36% (28)	30% (247)	N.S.

Note: Numbers in parentheses are the sample sizes on which the percentages are based.
* Significant at the .05 level. ** Significant at the .01 level. *** Significant at the .001 level.
N.S. = not significant.

percent of suburban movers had high social/physical problem index scores,
compared with three-fifths of returnees (63 percent) and one-half (49 percent) of local movers (table 3.12).

Similarly, suburban movers scored significantly higher than local
movers or returnees with respect to the neighborhood accessibility index.
They were more likely to report that their new neighborhoods had more
convenient shopping and better job opportunities than did the areas where
they had originally lived (table 3.12). Whereas half the suburban movers
scored high (six or more) on this index, only 20 percent of the returnees
and 15 percent of the local movers did so (table 3.12).

In the past, critics of housing mobility programs have argued that a
major disadvantage of moving to a low-poverty or suburban neighborhood

TABLE 3.11

Rotated Component Matrix: "Comparing your current neighborhood to your old one, in which one do you think you would be more likely to. . . ."

Characteristic	Worse with Respect to Social and Physical Conditions	Better with Respect to Accessibility	Better with Respect to the Social Environment
Find people who know each other	0.131	−0.101	0.719[a]
Find people who have jobs	−0.652[a]	0.413	0.216
Find people who use drugs	0.775[a]	−0.240	−0.032
Find houses that are rundown	0.758[a]	−0.331	−0.043
Find people who help each other when there is trouble	−0.383	0.233	0.678[a]
Find people who watch each other's children	−0.350	0.156	0.681[a]
Find people who are on welfare	0.815[a]	0.111	−0.026
Find violent gangs	0.780[a]	−0.215	−0.018
Find shopping that is convenient	−0.106	0.764[a]	0.056
Easily see friends and relatives	0.057	0.010	0.541[a]
Find better job opportunities	−0.216	0.798[a]	0.009
Find better schools	−0.495[a]	0.495	0.080

[a]These numbers are for questions loading highest on that component. "Find better schools" (inverse) was assigned to the worse social problems factor rather than the better accessibility one because it fit more logically into the former dimension.

is the loss of strong family and friendship ties. Briggs (2003) notes, however, that although strong social ties at inner-city locations may help low-income householders cope with difficult circumstances, these ties may not help residents move toward self-sufficiency. By implication, some social ties in the new neighborhood may be more helpful than comparable ties in distressed neighborhoods.

Our results show no significant differences between the three mover groups in the social environment scale, indicating that suburban movers were not hurt as a result of their move as measured by this indicator. The proportion of suburban movers with relatively high scores (nine or more, 58 percent) was only slightly higher than for returnees (53 percent), but was somewhat higher than for local movers (45 percent, as given in table 3.12). Suburban movers were just as likely as local movers to observe improvements in social networks (e.g., neighborhood people who know one another, residents watching out for neighbors' children).

TABLE 3.12

Scores on Social and Physical Problems Index, Neighborhood
Accessibility Index, and Social Environment Index, by Mobility Group

| | Mobility Status | | | | |
	Local Movers	Suburban-Bound Movers	Returnees	All Mobility Groups	Signif-icance
Index					
Social and physical problems index score					
3 or less	50.6%	84.6%	36.7%	66.9%	***
4 or more	49.4%	15.4%	63.3%	33.1%	
N =	85	130	30	245	
Neighborhood accessibility index score					
5 or less	84.7%	49.6%	80.0%	65.4%	***
6 or more	15.3%	50.4%	20.0%	34.6%	
N =	85	131	30	246	
Social environment index score					
8 or less	55.3%	42.0%	46.7%	47.2%	N.S.
9 or more	44.7%	58.0%	53.3%	52.8%	
N =	85	131	30	246	

* Significant at the .05 level. ** Significant at the .01 level. *** Significant at the .001 level.
N.S. = not significant.

Self-Sufficiency

Table 3.13, based on a simple bivariate analysis, shows that both suburban movers and returnees were more likely to become employed than local movers and nonmovers. This implies that the exposure to the suburban job market may have helped in getting and holding a job. However, when we controlled for the impact of relevant variables (including access to an automobile and satisfaction with the Section 8 briefing session), suburban movers were not more likely than other types of movers or nonmovers to be employed at the time of the 1999 telephone interview (logistic regression results are not included here). There were also insignificant differences among the four groups in the reasons provided by the respondents for shifting from being unemployed to becoming employed. Regardless of mobility group, respondents who started working typically mentioned either that they were self-motivated (e.g., they wanted to become more self-sufficient) or that they had responded to financial needs (e.g., they wanted to better support their family).

The bivariate results provide no evidence that suburban movers were more likely than others to move off welfare (table 3.13). The proportion of suburban movers making this type of shift (37 percent) was only slightly higher than for local movers—the next highest group (34 percent). The logistic regression results (not included here) also showed that suburban movers were more, not less, likely than others to be receiving welfare at the time of the 1999 survey, all other factors held constant. Those who were receiving welfare at the time they joined the voucher program, those who found the Section 8 briefing session very useful, and those who had one or more children were most likely to be receiving welfare in 1999. Although there were no statistically significant differences by mover group in reasons for moving off welfare, suburban movers were somewhat more likely to cite their own self-motivation.

Why is it that moving to suburban Alameda County had so little impact on employment status and welfare status? We suspect that there are two reasons. First, the impact of welfare reform in moving people off welfare and into jobs might have been so great that it is hard to detect any additional impact due to a suburban location. Second, the insignificant results may reflect the fact that in the San Francisco area, the spatial mismatch theory is not valid. That is, there may be sufficient jobs in downtown Oakland, Berkeley, and nearby San Francisco (aided by an efficient public transit system) so that inner-city residents are as accessible to jobs as residents of southern Alameda County.

Mobility Desires

The inclination to move provides another indicator of residential satisfaction, because families that are satisfied with their housing usually are not inclined to move. Respondents were asked, "How interested are you in moving to a different house or apartment?" Forty-one percent of all movers said they were very interested in moving, while 17 percent were somewhat interested. Ten percent were not very interested in moving, and 32 percent said they were not interested at all. Given the high level of housing dissatisfaction among returnees, it is perhaps not surprising that of the three groups of movers, they were most likely to be interested in moving (68 percent). Similarly small proportions of suburban movers (36 percent) and local movers (40 percent) expressed interest in moving.

Fifty-nine percent of all respondents cited housing conditions as their

TABLE 3.13

Changes in Employment Status and Welfare Status: Differences by Mobility Status

		Mobility Status				
Characteristic	*Non-movers*	*Local Movers*	*Suburban-Bound Movers*	*Returnees*	*All Mobility Groups*	*Signif-icance*
Employment status at original location						
Employed	29.3%	18.6%	21.5%	23.3%	21.8%	**
Unemployed	9.8%	27.8%	26.2%	23.3%	24.2%	
Disabled or retired	48.8%	32.0%	22.3%	16.7%	28.5%	
In school or homemaker	12.2%	21.6%	30.0%	36.7%	28.5%	
N =	41	97	130	30	298	
Employment status at current location						
Employed	20.0%	24.0%	47.0%	50.0%	36.2%	**
Unemployed	5.0%	14.6%	8.3%	10.0%	10.1%	
Disabled or retired	67.5%	52.1%	34.8%	30.0%	44.3%	
In school or homemaker	7.5%	9.4%	9.8%	10.0%	9.4%	
N =	40	96	132	30	298	
Change in employment status between original and current location						
Employed at both points	10.0%	10.4%	16.2%	20.0%	13.9%	**
Unemployed at both points	60.0%	67.7%	46.9%	46.7%	55.4%	
Employed, then unemployed	20.0%	8.3%	5.4%	3.3%	8.1%	
Unemployed, then employed	10.0%	13.5%	31.5%	30.0%	22.6%	
N =	40	96	130	30	296	
Reason respondent shifted from unemployed to employed						
"Just got a job" or entered training program	25.0%	7.7%	4.9%	0.0%	6.0%	N.S.
Financial need	50.0%	38.5%	29.3%	22.2%	31.3%	
Felt motivated to work	25.0%	46.2%	39.0%	66.7%	43.3%	
In school before	0.0%	0.0%	14.6%	0.0%	9.0%	
Other	0.0%	7.7%	12.2%	11.1%	10.5%	
N =	4	13	41	9	67	

(continued)

main reason for wanting to move—they needed more space, wanted a newer unit, or wanted to buy a house. Fifteen percent cited problems with landlords (e.g., the landlord doesn't fix anything), while 14 percent mentioned neighborhood problems—the neighborhood was beginning to deteriorate, or they wanted to get away from drugs. Two percent cited the Section 8 program itself (e.g., the landlord is getting out of the program). The remaining 10 percent mentioned personal changes, such as having had another child. Suburban movers were significantly more likely to want

TABLE 3.13 (continued)

| | Mobility Status | | | | |
Characteristic	Non-movers	Local Movers	Suburban-Bound Movers	Returnees	All Mobility Groups	Significance
Welfare status at original location: Receive AFDC/TANF						
Yes	26.8%	58.3%	62.1%	60.0%	55.9%	***
No	73.2%	41.7%	37.9%	40.0%	44.1%	
N =	41	96	132	30	299	
Welfare status at current location: Receive AFDC/TANF						
Yes	5.0%	26.0%	25.8%	30.0%	23.5%	*
No	95.0%	74.0%	74.2%	70.0%	76.5%	
N =	40	96	132	30	298	
Change in welfare status between original and current location						
On welfare at both points	2.5%	24.2%	24.2%	30.0%	21.9%	
Off welfare at both points	70.0%	40.0%	36.4%	40.0%	42.4%	*
On welfare, then off welfare	25.0%	33.7%	37.9%	30.0%	34.0%	
Off welfare, then on welfare	2.5%	2.1%	1.5%	0.0%	1.7%	
N =	40	95	132	30	297	
Reason why shifted off welfare						
Motivation	33.3%	46.4%	63.3%	55.6%	54.7%	N.S.
Personal changes	55.6%	35.7%	12.2%	22.2%	24.4%	
Went on another support program	11.1%	10.7%	8.2%	0.0%	8.4%	
To improve financial condition	0.0%	0.0%	6.1%	11.1%	4.2%	
Other	0.0%	7.2%	10.2%	11.1%	8.5%	
N =	9	28	49	8	95	

*Significant at the .05 level. **Significant at the .01 level. ***Significant at the .001 level.
N.S. = not significant.

to move for housing reasons. It appears that many suburban movers sought to relocate not because they were dissatisfied but because they sought to move toward their housing ideal.

What Types of Movers Were Most Likely to Be Satisfied with the Housing Search and to Perceive Improvements in Housing and Neighborhood Conditions?

The results reported thus far describe the differences in satisfaction expressed by suburban movers, local movers, and returnees with respect to their housing search and perceived changes in residential conditions. The descriptive analyses, however, do not control for the socioeconomic and demographic differences that existed among the three groups (suburban movers, for example, had higher incomes). A question that arises is whether, after taking into account the demographic differences that existed among the three groups, mobility status played an important role in the experiences of residents in the housing market.

Housing Search

The logistic regression results (tables 3.2 and 3.3) provide no evidence that being a suburban mover contributed to either an increased or decreased likelihood of being satisfied with the housing search, either directly or indirectly. Mobility status was an insignificant predictor at all stages of the analysis. Six factors were significant predictors of satisfaction with the housing search, based on one or both sets of logistic regression runs: age, being a welfare recipient, believing that the Section 8 briefing session was very useful, perceiving discrimination in the housing search (negative), experiencing problems in exercising portability (negative), and believing that the housing search was somewhat or very difficult (negative). The one finding that was unanticipated was the significance of welfare status. We had assumed that welfare recipients would experience more difficulty in conducting their housing search and, as a result, would be more dissatisfied with it; instead, welfare recipients were more satisfied with their housing search.

Changes in Housing and Neighborhood Conditions

Table 3.1 shows that, compared with local movers and returnees, suburban movers were more likely to perceive improvements in their housing, neighborhood, and safety between their original and current location. It is possible that these results might have been influenced by the demographic characteristics of the suburban-bound movers, local movers, and returnees (e.g., differences in age, family composition, income). We speculated that even when these background characteristics were controlled, mobility status would still influence perceptions of changes in residential conditions.

Tables 3.4 and 3.5—which present the logistic regression result related to the determinants of perceived changes in housing and neighborhood conditions, and changes in neighborhood safety—support the latter hypothesis. Mobility status had a statistically significant impact on perceived changes in housing conditions, neighborhood conditions, and personal safety when background demographic factors were controlled. Suburban movers were about twice as likely as local movers (1.97) and four times as likely as returnees (4.23) to report that they had experienced improvements in housing conditions since receiving a housing voucher. [These results—1.97 and 4.23—are the "Exp(B)" statistics; for space reasons, they are not included in tables 3.2 through 3.5.] Similarly, suburban movers were 1.78 times more likely than local movers to report improvements in neighborhood conditions. Finally, suburban movers were more likely to report improvements in their perception of their personal safety when compared with families moving to other locations. Local movers were more than three times as likely (3.35) as suburban movers to perceive that crime conditions had gotten worse between their original and current location, and returnees were almost ten times as likely (9.80) as suburban movers to state that crime had gotten worse over the course of their moves.

Furthermore, when background demographic characteristics were controlled, suburban movers scored lower on the social and physical problems index and scored higher on the accessibility index. Specifically, suburban movers were about one-sixth (0.16) as likely to score high on the social and physical problems index as local movers and one-tenth (0.09) as likely to score high in comparison with returnees. Similarly, the probability of suburban movers to score high on the accessibiliy index was five times (5.46) that for local movers and more than four times (4.35) that for returnees. Finally, as was the case for the cross-tabular results, there were no significant differences by mobility status group with respect to the social environment index.

Conclusions

Two special housing mobility programs—the Gautreaux Assisted Housing Program and the Moving to Opportunity for Fair Housing Demonstration Program—have produced promising results in increasing locational choices and in promoting economic self-sufficiency. In contrast, research on the regular operation of the Section 8 voucher program has produced much less encouraging findings with respect to the program's enhancing locational choices. Voucher participants have often made short-distance moves and have reclustered in high-poverty, highly segregated neighborhoods in the central city.

Given the above, the situation in Alameda County has stood out as an anomaly. As of 2000, about one-tenth (approximately 1,200 families) of the Section 8 families in the East Bay Area had relocated to the newer suburban areas under the jurisdiction of the HACA, the housing authority serving the newer, more suburban parts of the county.

Although previous writings on the Section 8 program imply that suburban movers will experience greater difficulties carrying out their housing search than will local movers, our results based on an analysis of a survey of 300 Alameda County voucher recipients did not support this hypothesis. Relatively few suburban movers experienced racial discrimination, and most said they were happy with their housing search. Furthermore, there was no evidence that suburban movers were more likely to perceive difficulties in the housing search or to be more dissatisfied with the housing search when other characteristics were held constant.

Consistent with earlier research, this chapter has shown that these city–suburban moves have led to improvements in housing and neighborhood conditions. Suburban movers experienced greater improvements than local movers by moving into areas with more racial and ethnic diversity, higher income levels, and higher housing values. Furthermore, when asked to compare their current location with their original one, suburban movers were more likely than local movers or returnees to (1) report that their current home and neighborhood were better; (2) feel safer at their current location; (3) observe better social and physical conditions at their current location (more people with jobs, better schools, fewer people using drugs, fewer rundown houses); and (4) praise their current neighborhood's accessibility to shopping and job opportunities. And in contrast to what some critics have asserted, suburban-bound families were able to experience these improvements without meaningful problems of adjustment at their new suburban location.

Notes

1. The Gautreaux Housing Program and the Moving to Opportunity demonstration program have been able to achieve spatial deconcentration of low-

income families through extensive counseling and support services and special geographical requirements dealing with where voucher recipients could move. Alameda County's migration, however, has been accomplished through the normal administration of the Section 8 rental voucher and rental certificate programs.

2. The focus of this chapter is on the ability of low-income families to look for and find homes in the suburbs. This might lead some readers to the mistaken impression that Alameda County's suburbs are socioeconomically homogeneous. The reality is quite different. The Alameda suburbs are socioeconomically heterogeneous. In 1989, the median household income in the areas outside of Oakland and Berkeley ranged from $27,626 in Ashland to $84,498 in Piedmont (Alameda County Planning Department 1992). Our focus on the ability to move to "the suburbs" is justifiable because in the past the city/suburban boundary has been viewed by many as a formidable barrier for low-income and minority families. Ideally, we would have liked to compare the housing search experiences of households moving into different Alameda County suburbs. However, the limited number of suburban movers in our sample precluded a separate analysis of migration patterns into particular localities.

3. It is important to emphasize that these two concepts—the difficulty of the search, and satisfaction with the search—are really quite different. Whereas the difficulty of the search is related only to the housing search process, satisfaction with the search takes into account the results of the search as well as the process of searching.

4. For a detailed discussion of the survey methodology, see Varady and Walker (2000b). Answers from the open-ended questions (the "verbatims") were postcoded by trained coders, and the resulting variables were analyzed (along with the results from the closed-ended questions) using the SPSS Inc. package. In addition, we created an Excel file by merging the SPSS data set (including the recoded verbatims) with the verbatims, using the respondents' identification numbers as a basis for the linkage. We then sorted and examined the verbatims for particular groups (e.g., suburban movers, local movers), using the SphinxSurvey software distributed by Scolari/Sage Publications.

5. The sample frame was a merged database, which was obtained by combining records on all families receiving housing vouchers from the Oakland, Berkeley, and Alameda County housing authorities. This sample frame provided information on the distribution of the Section 8 voucher population by mobility status.

6. Suburban movers and returnees were oversampled to provide sufficient numbers in these groups for cross-tabular and regression analysis. Because we were using the sample for analytic rather than descriptive purposes, we chose not to weight the data for the statistical analysis. Among all voucher recipients (i.e., all those in the merged database, which contained all the records of families receiving housing vouchers from the three housing authorities), 59 percent were nonmovers, 29 percent were local movers, 10 percent were suburban movers, and 2 percent were returnees from suburban Alameda to Oakland or Berkeley (Varady and Walker 2000b).

7. Logistic regression analysis was carried out in three stages. The first stage was limited to demographic/housing characteristics plus mobility status only. In the second stage, we added housing search characteristics (including evaluations of the importance of the Section 8 briefing session) to those included in stage one. Stage three included demographic/housing characteristics plus mobility status plus housing search characteristics plus the perceived difficulty of the housing search. The reason for carrying out the logistic regression runs in three stages was to determine whether mobility status had an indirect impact on satisfaction with the housing search. If it had had such an impact, mobility status would have been significantly correlated with search satisfaction at stage one but would have dropped out as significant in stages two and three. A fourth regression run was limited to variables that had been shown to be statistically significant with the third set of variables. Two versions of the above four-stage logistic analysis were prepared. The first version was based on the full sample of movers but did not include an index measuring the number of portability problems. The second included this index, and as a result, it was limited to suburban movers and returnees.

8. Most of the Alameda County voucher recipients in our survey sample moved in during the early and middle 1990s at a time when the prevalence of affordable housing units in better neighborhoods made the suburban part of the county attractive to families with vouchers seeking to improve their housing and neighborhood conditions. These families were suburbanizing because of the availability of affordable units and not because housing was cheaper on the suburban side of the city/suburban boundary. Berkeley and Oakland had the lowest median rents of municipalities in Alameda County in 1990 ($426 and $538, respectively) as compared with $626, the median for the county as a whole) (U.S. Census 1990 data, as cited in Alameda County Planning Department 1991). It should be noted that rents varied widely among suburban Alameda County jurisdictions, ranging from $650 in San Leandro (next to Oakland) to $1,001 in Piedmont (a high-income enclave surrounded by the city of Oakland). Thus, although we treat the Alameda suburbs as a single entity in much of this chapter, we are aware of the socioeconomic differences within the county. The market has also changed over the years. From late 1999 to mid-2002, the housing market tightened considerably. With a vacancy rate of less than 2 percent, portability stopped because few voucher recipients, including those served by HACA, were finding units. HACA's success rate was about 23 percent during this period. By November 2002, the housing market had softened, and the incidence of portability had increased as well. HACA was averaging 60 voucher recipients per month coming into its jurisdiction to look for units (Basgal 2002b).

9. These results are based on the file created by merging the three housing authorities' client databases. See note 5 above.

10. The designations of the neighborhoods and their boundaries were defined in consultation with the planning and community development departments in Oakland and Berkeley.

11. See Varady and Walker (2000a) for a detailed discussion of the characteristics of these Alameda County communities.

12. Initially, however, the Berkeley Housing Authority tried to limit portability by erecting administrative barriers. This section draws on open-ended interviews conducted with housing officials in the East Bay area. For more on the relationships between the Alameda County housing authorities, see Varady and Walker (2000b).

13. HACA scored 89 (90 is a high performer) in HUD's Section 8 Management Assessment Program for the 2001 fiscal year. Furthermore, in 1996, HACA received a HUD award for sustained excellence in the management of the Section 8 program under the HUD Office of Public and Indian Housing's 1996 Performance Awards Program. Ophelia Basgal, executive director of HACA, is extremely well respected, both locally and nationally, and has been a driving force for the effective implementation of regional approaches to portability.

14. A housing authority may bill a sending housing authority for reimbursement of the housing assistance payments made to the landlord on behalf of an incoming family, or it may "absorb" the family into its own Section 8 program.

15. Blakely (2002); also, Euston (1998).

16. It is possible that compared with voucher recipients in the West, voucher recipients living in Eastern and Midwestern cities (1) assess differently the advantages and disadvantages of living in the central city versus the suburbs, and (2) have different preferences for living in the central city versus the suburbs. Sigelman and Henig (2001) conducted a study in the Washington area on central city versus suburban preferences. Although a broad transracial consensus existed about the strengths and weaknesses of living in the city versus the suburbs, blacks and whites seemed to stress these factors differently in formulating general preferences as to where to live. Whether the authors' findings are generalizable to Western metropolitan areas is unknown.

17. Respondents were asked: "Overall, how important was the briefing session you attended when you got your Section 8 (voucher/certificate) in helping you with your housing search. Would you say it was: (1) very helpful, (2) somewhat helpful, (3) not very helpful, or (4) not at all helpful?"

18. Our results differ sharply from those obtained by Popkin and Cunningham (2000, 28) in their Chicago Section 8 study. Both successful and unsuccessful searchers complained about the briefing. "The briefings were too long, very complex, and were difficult to understand."

19. Our results showing Alameda County Section 8 recipients indifferent to the race of their neighbors are quite different from those obtained by Squires, Friedman, and Saidat (2001) in their Washington, D.C., study. They found that blacks were significantly more likely than whites to prefer a neighborhood that was mixed or where blacks constituted a majority of residents. Only about 1 in 4 whites and 1 in 10 blacks claimed that the number of blacks present in a neighborhood did not matter to them in deciding upon an ideal neighborhood in which to live. The differences in results between the two studies may reflect variations

in the wording of the question or the fact that West Coast Section 8 voucher recipients are more indifferent to the racial composition of their surrounding neighborhood than either whites or blacks in the Washington area. Given the data at hand, it is impossible to test for the validity of these two alternative explanations.

20. Although differences in wording make comparisons impossible, it is interesting to compare our results on perceptions of housing discrimination with the results from two recent studies. Squires, Friedman, and Saidat (2001) asked respondents if they had encountered any form of racial discrimination within the past three years in their efforts to obtain housing or mortgage loans. Black respondents were more than five times more likely than whites to say that they had experienced discrimination, 11 vs. 2 percent. Abravanel and Cunningham (2002), in a national study, found that 14 percent of the adult public claimed to have experienced some form of housing discrimination at one point or another in their lives. We are aware that questions on self-reported discrimination may not be fully reliable for several reasons: (1) Some people may not know that they experienced it; (2) some landlords may use Section 8 status as a proxy for race; and (3) other landlords may discriminate against home seekers on the basis of the racial composition of the previous neighborhood, a form of racial discrimination. Nevertheless, taking these three factors into account does not refute our main conclusion that overt racial discrimination was relatively uncommon for these movers in Alameda County. Our informant interviews (discussed above) and a housing audit conducted by Eden Council for Hope and Opportunity (n.d., 9) provides additional support for our conclusion. For additional discussion of housing discrimination, see the Alameda County HOME Consortium report (1995, 44).

21. Our results on access to an automobile are broadly similar to those of an HACA survey carried out in early 2002 about the method of transportation people used to come into the HACA office. About four-fifths came by car, either their own or someone else's. The remainder used BART or the area's extensive bus system (Basgal 2002a). Again, our results for Alameda County are sharply different from those obtained by Popkin and Cunningham (2000) for Chicago Section 8 recipients. Whereas in our Alameda County survey sample, most Section 8 recipients who moved had access to a car, in Chicago, few had cars; consequently, most relied on public transportation and many mentioned that lack of transportation was a barrier to looking for housing, particularly in the suburbs. There are two possible explanations for the differences between our findings and Popkin and Cunningham's. Because Chicago's voucher population was needier, this would explain lower levels of auto ownership. Conversely, the differences might reflect the greater reliance on public transportation in Chicago than in Alameda County.

22. It is widely believed that having a car leads to an easier housing search. However, despite the fact that many of the Alameda voucher recipients who exercised portability had access to a car, a large proportion in this group said that they experienced serious problems traveling around. This seeming contradiction

may reflect the possibility that some of those who said that they had access to a car did not own one but were relying on cars owned by friends and relatives. Furthermore, given the distances and traffic, searching for housing in suburban Alameda County probably was difficult with or without a car.

23. Although this chapter focuses on the perceptions and assessments of voucher recipients, it highlights the importance of housing market conditions in influencing the difficulty of the housing search.

24. In general, Alameda County movers were more satisfied with the housing search than were movers interviewed in the four-city vouchering-out study (Varady and Walker 1998, 2000a). Eighty-nine percent of the movers interviewed for the Alameda study were somewhat or very satisfied with the search compared with only 61 percent in the vouchering-out study. Three possible explanations for these differences seem plausible. First, voucher recipients in the vouchering-out study were living in subsidized housing developments and likely had less experience with the private housing market than recipients in Alameda County. Second, unlike the Alameda County voucher holders, the vouchered-out residents were given no choice; they had to move out of their housing developments. Third, it is possible that voucher recipients in Alameda County received better assistance from the local housing authorities than was true for the voucher holders in the four-city vouchering-out study.

25. This respondent expanded on the reasons for choosing her new location: "I liked this area because I no longer interacted with the people I used to when I was using drugs. It was a good area. [It was] closer to the markets and transportation. . . . I am much happier. I get along with my neighbors. I am across the street from the school, so I am closer to my kids. The shopping is closer. Everything I need is right here."

26. For each specific characteristic, respondents were asked whether that characteristic was more likely to be found in the current neighborhood (coded "3"), whether it was more likely to be found in the original neighborhood ("1"), or whether the characteristic was equally likely to be found in the original and the current neighborhood ("2"). In response to some of the comparisons, a meaningful number of respondents said "don't know." To minimize the number of cases lost due to missing information, the "don't know" responses were coded as "2."

4

Toward a Realistic Housing Voucher Policy

When the U.S. Department of Housing and Urban Development (HUD) introduced housing vouchers in the early 1980s, they were to be part of a broader poverty deconcentration strategy that also included efforts to disperse federally subsidized private housing and scattered-site public housing in the suburbs. During the 1990s, mixed-income inner-city developments, such as the HOPE VI public housing revitalization, were added as a second mechanism for deconcentrating poverty.

Our literature review (chapter 1) showed that housing mobility programs are not a panacea for urban poverty. The Gautreaux and Moving to Opportunity for Fair Housing Demonstration (MTO) programs have produced some positive results. However, these are small-scale programs that cannot easily be expanded into national programs. In addition, research on social mixing provides little support for the role model and social network hypotheses; the presumed benefits are unlikely to occur because many of those moving from the inner city have relatively little in common with their middle-income neighbors. Research at the national and local levels on the operation of the regular Section 8 program highlights the problems facing voucher holders, but it also shows that well-managed programs can lead to meaningful improvements in housing and neighborhood conditions.

A housing mobility strategy based on an improved Section 8 voucher program would offer advantages over the implementation of a massive MTO-type effort. It would be more politically practical. It would be

159

cheaper (i.e., more people could be assisted with a limited amount of funding). It would provide the poor with options; they would not be required to move to areas meeting particular criteria. And, finally, although it might not address some of the root causes of urban poverty such as the breakdown of the family unit, it would promote improvement in housing and neighborhood conditions, a modest but nevertheless important goal.

Alexander von Hoffman (1998) wisely indicates the need to lower expectations about what housing mobility programs can accomplish:

> The simple goal of providing decent and safe housing to low-income people where they now live [or where they want to live; *phrase added*] is not as lofty as creating modern housing, a high-rise civilization, or a socially heterogeneous society. Yet it is just as worthy and, in these perilous times for social policy, has the advantage of being remotely possible. (p. 19)

In writing this book, we have sought to add to the limited literature on the experiences of voucher recipients in the regular Section 8 program; a disproportionate amount of existing scholarly work deals with the Gautreaux and MTO programs. Two empirical studies constitute the core of this book: (1) a four-city comparative case study of families forced to move from severely distressed, subsidized private developments in Baltimore, Newport News, Kansas City, and San Francisco; and (2) a case study of the operation of the voucher programs in Alameda County, California. These studies suggest two important lessons for housing policy.

First, it is important to develop realistic goals for the vouchering out of distressed subsidized private developments or distressed public housing developments. Our four-city vouchering out study showed that although many of the displaced residents chose to remain in the same area, most improved their situation by moving. The overwhelming majority were satisfied with their new homes and neighborhoods, and most said that they were more satisfied with their new homes and neighborhoods than they had been with their former ones. However, most of the families continued to live in racially segregated areas.

Thus, it may be unreasonable to expect many families that are forced to move and are given vouchers—particularly those relying on public transportation—to relocate to new and unfamiliar neighborhoods without support, or without intensive counseling encouraging them to do so. If residential integration is to be a high-priority goal, four programmatic changes would be necessary in HUD's current approach to vouchering out.

First, it would be necessary to move away from reliance on lists of Section 8 landlords and to attract many more new landlords to the program. Second, householders would need to be provided with more assistance in looking for suitable housing; in some cases, it might be necessary for counselors to accompany the voucher recipients. Third, unlike the voluntary counseling provided at vouchered-out properties, it might be necessary to institute MTO-type intensive counseling, emphasizing areas such as self-sufficiency, tenant housekeeping, and preparation for meetings with landlords. And fourth, to achieve residential integration, it probably would be necessary to require residents to move to "nonimpacted areas."

Applying more intensive MTO-type counseling to situations like the vouchering-out effort is, however, no easy matter. First, there is the matter of cost. The vouchering-out counseling cost in our study ranged from $348 to $500 per family; the average counseling cost to help an MTO family find a unit was $3,077 (Basgal and Villarreal 2001). Second, HUD would have to be prepared to reproduce MTO's counseling and relocation requirements, which may not be appropriate in all cases. MTO is a voluntary program. When people sign up for this program, they understand that the voucher or certificate comes with these strings. The situation for vouchered-out residents, like those in this study, is quite different. These were people who just happened to live in a distressed property that had to be closed. HUD needs to be cautious in imposing requirements on them. As Donna Kelley (1996), HUD's asset manager at Eutaw Gardens, stated in an interview, "It sounds awfully Big Brotherish to say, 'Because you live in Eutaw Gardens you must now be an MTO person.'"

Adding income or racial deconcentration as goals would immensely complicate any large-scale vouchering out. The benefits of requiring tenants to move to low-poverty or low-minority neighborhoods would have to be weighed against the less expensive moves to known neighborhoods agreeable to most families and against allowing voucher recipients the freedom of choice to use it. This dilemma—whether HUD should take on the additional goals of poverty and racial deconcentration, given the pressures on HUD to demolish the most distressed public and private units and to relocate residents as quickly as possible—will not be easily resolved.

The second lesson is that housing vouchers work far better in some places than others and that it is important to recognize the variations in program effectiveness that exist. Alameda County, California, is an example of a metropolitan area where people can and do choose to make moves to the suburbs without special housing mobility programs involving intensive counseling and/or geographical restrictions imposed on them. Oakland voucher recipients who crossed into the more suburban parts of Alameda County experienced no more difficulty in searching for and finding a home than those who moved within Oakland. Furthermore, suburban movers were significantly more likely to perceive improvements in housing and neighborhood conditions than local movers.

The preceding suggests that it is a mistake to develop a "one size fits all" voucher policy for the country. That is, it is inappropriate to develop voucher policy only on the basis of research on places like Chicago, where residents experience considerable difficulty when they attempt to relocate. Turner's (1998, 390) proposal to supplement the Section 8 program with intensive housing counseling and search assistance may not be required in places like Alameda County.

High-performing housing authorities should be given the flexibility to allocate funds as they see fit. In other words, there is no reason to replicate elements of the MTO program nationally, with the type of requirements placed on the experimental group for intensive counseling and restrictions on where vouchers can be used, if cheaper, more effective approaches are available. Furthermore, when local housing authorities are able to rely on the regular operation of the Section 8 program, recipients are able to exercise free choice, something they would not be able to do if the restrictions applied to the MTO experimental group were required.

The three housing authorities in the East Bay Area examined in the Alameda County case study have shown that it is possible to develop effective collaborative relationships that promote wider locational choices. Consequently, it may not be necessary to replace the current balkanized system of administration of Section 8 vouchers in particular metropolitan areas with regional administration (Basgal and Villarreal 2001; Katz and Turner 2001).

Although suburban-bound Section 8 voucher recipients in Alameda County did benefit through improved residential conditions, many experienced difficulty in carrying out their housing search. For example, many complained about the lack of affordable housing and about the unwillingness of landlords to accept Section 8 vouchers. To address the problem of discrimination due to Section 8 status, localities should consider passing and enforcing some type of protection against discrimination of potential renters based on receipt of housing assistance. To address the problem of access to affordable housing opportunities, local housing authorities should expand landlord outreach efforts and encourage more landlords to rent to families in the Section 8 program. They should also provide more extensive listings of suitable homes to families. However, housing authorities need to manage their programs effectively to convince property owners in desirable neighborhoods to participate.

Policymakers should devote more attention to "returnees," families who initially make city-to-suburban moves but later move back to their original locality. The respondents in the survey sample who returned to Oakland or Berkeley did so for a variety of reasons: They were dissatisfied with the housing and neighborhood conditions in the suburban location; they were able to find better conditions at a location in Oakland or Berkeley; or they had an unsuccessful search when looking for new housing in the suburbs. Among the three mover groups, returnees were least likely to report improvements in housing and neighborhood conditions when comparing their original and current locations. Assisting Section 8 families that want to remain in the suburbs ought to be a high priority for housing officials, but when families who move back have good reasons for doing so, these should be respected. Follow-up services should focus on helping families become stable in their new communities and develop better relationships with their landlords (Cunningham et al. 2002).

It would be incorrect to interpret our results to indicate that everyone should be moving to the suburbs to find better housing and neighborhood conditions. In many cities, a move of a few blocks can lead to better housing conditions and greater safety (Varady and Walker 2000a; Varady, Walker, and Wang 2001). Just getting out of distressed public housing, or distressed publicly subsidized private housing, or substandard private housing can make a big difference. And for some, the best option might be to remain in place, having the owner bring the home up to housing quality standards. The mission of federal housing policy should be to promote opportunities for families to move into better housing—particularly, into better housing in low-poverty neighborhoods, if that is a family's desire.

An improved Section 8 voucher program could therefore make a modest contribution, especially in places like Alameda County, California, to reducing patterns of income and racial segregation. However, it is important to recognize that tenant-based subsidies are only one part of a comprehensive strategy needed to cure segregation and to mitigate the high costs of residential segregation (Briggs 2003). Other key elements include inclusionary housing, fair share housing policies, fair housing enforcement, scattered-site public housing, and community development (including mixed-income development, to attract diverse in-movers), school desegregation by mandatory busing or magnet schools, fiscal reform to equalize public services across municipal boundaries, reverse commuting to suburban jobs, and regional workforce development alliances or networks.

Appendix: The Housing Choice Voucher Program

The fundamental eligibility requirement for participation in the voucher program is income. (The information in this appendix on the Housing Choice Voucher Program draws on HUD 2001.) Eligibility is determined by the local public housing authority (PHA) based on a family's total annual gross income and family size. In general, a family's income may not exceed 50 percent of the median income for the county or metropolitan area in which the family chooses to live. Three-fourths of vouchers are reserved for extremely low-income families—those at or below 30 percent of area median income.

Housing voucher recipients are required to pay 30 percent of their monthly-adjusted gross income for rent and utilities; the government subsidizes the balance of the costs up to a locally determined maximum, or payment standard. Payment standards are set by the PHA, based on fair market rents (FMRs) that are designated annually by HUD for housing markets throughout the country. FMRs reflect the rent and utilities charged in a particular housing market for a typical, nonluxury unit (adjusted by unit size). FMRs are usually 40 percent of an area's median rent.

After receiving a voucher, a family usually has 120 days to find a unit. Once a unit is selected, the PHA makes an inspection to ensure that it meets housing quality standards, then reviews the lease before approving the unit for rental by the participant and checks that the rent is reasonable. A voucher recipient may select a unit with a rent that is below or above the payment standard. If it costs more than the payment standard, the family is required to pay the difference, but the family may not pay more than 40 percent of its income for housing costs. The PHA pays the rent subsidy directly to the landlord on behalf of the participating family;

the family pays the difference between the actual rent charged by the land-lord and the amount subsidized by the program.

The housing choice voucher program is designed to allow families to move anywhere in the United States, providing that the family lives in the jurisdiction of the PHA issuing the voucher when the family applies for assistance. Portability is the mechanism by which Section 8 recipients can move from one PHA's jurisdiction to another. It is an important tool in helping families move to neighborhoods offering better opportunities and improved living environments.

References

Abravanel, Martin D., and Mary K. Cunningham. 2002. *How much do we know? Public awareness of the nation's fair housing laws.* Prepared by the Urban Institute. Washington, DC: U.S. Department of Housing and Urban Development.

Alameda County HOME Consortium. 1995. *Consolidated plan FY1995–FY1999 for the Alameda HOME Consortium,* June. Hayward, CA: Alameda County HOME Consortium.

Alameda County Planning Department. 1991. *1990 census housing characteristics: Alameda County.* Pub. No. 91–6. Hayward, CA: Alameda County Planning Department.

———. 1992. *1990 census household, family and per capita income, Alameda County and its cities.* Pub. No. 92–3. Hayward, CA: Alameda County Planning Department.

Alltucker, Ken. 2002. 30 Years of undermining neighborhoods: Section 8 program concentrated the poor in a few areas. *Cincinnati Enquirer* (February 25): local news. http://enquirer.com/editions/2002/02/25/loc_30_years_of.html.

Atkinson, Rowland, and Keith Kintrea. 1999. *Reconnecting excluded communities: The neighborhood impacts of owner occupation.* Report to Scottish Homes. Edinburgh: Scottish Homes.

Barton, Stephen. 1999. Acting director, Housing and Community Development Department, City of Berkeley, CA. Personal interview conducted by David Varady and Carole C. Walker, December 9.

Basgal, Ophelia. 2002a. Executive director, Housing Authority of Alameda County, CA. E-mail correspondence to David P. Varady, October 17.

———. 2002b. E-mail correspondence to David P. Varady, October 29.

Basgal, Ophelia, and Joseph Villarreal. 2001. Comment on Bruce J. Katz and Margery Austin Turner's "Who should run the housing voucher program? A reform proposal": Why public housing authorities remain the best solution for running the housing voucher program. *Housing Policy Debate* 12, 2: 263–81.

Blakely, Edward. 2002. Former member of the City of Oakland Housing Development Corporation and policy adviser to the mayor of Oakland. E-mail correspondence to David P. Varady, October 15.

Briggs, Xavier de Souza. 2003. Desegregating the city: Space and inequality in global perspective. Unpublished paper. Harvard University, John F. Kennedy School of Government, Cambridge, MA.

Brophy, Paul C., and Rhonda N. Smith. 1997. Mixed-income housing: Factors for success. *Cityscape* 3, 2: 3–32.

Buron, Larry, Sandra Nolden, Kathleen Heinz, and Julie Stewart. 2000. *Assessment of the economic and social characteristics of LIHTC residential neighborhoods.* Washington, DC: U.S. Department of Housing and Urban Development.

Campbell DeLong Resources Inc. 1998. *Keeping drug activity out of rental property: A police guide for establishing landlord training programs.* Washington, DC: Bureau of Justice Assistance, U.S. Department of Justice.

City of Oakland, California. 1998. *Community and economic development: Envision Oakland, CA. City of Oakland general plan,* March.

Crystal, Ruth. 1996. Program Director, Community Action Network, Moving to Opportunity. Personal interview conducted by David P. Varady, Baltimore, May 29.

Cunningham, Mary K., Susan J. Popkin, Janet L. Smith, and Anne Knepler. 2002. *CHAC mobility counseling assessment. Final report.* Submitted to the MacArthur Foundation. Washington, DC: Urban Institute.

Cunningham, Mary K., David J. Sylvester, and Margery A. Turner. 2000. *Section 8 families in the Washington region: Neighborhood choices and constraints.* Report by the Urban Institute to the Metropolitan Washington Council of Governments. Washington, DC: Urban Institute.

Davis, Harold. 1998. Former director, Oakland Housing Authority. Personal interview conducted by Carole C. Walker, November 10.

Devine, Deborah J., Robert W. Gray, Lester Rubin, and Lydia B. Taghavi. 2003. *Housing choice voucher location patterns: Implications for participants and neighborhood welfare.* Washington, DC: U.S. Department of Housing and Urban Development.

Eden Council for Hope and Opportunity. n.d. *Fair housing audit report 1998–1999 covering unincorporated southern Alameda County, Hayward, Union City, San Leandro, and Livermore.* Alameda County, CA: Eden Council for Hope and Opportunity.

Ellen, Ingrid Gould, and Margery Austin Turner. 1997. Does neighborhood matter? Assessing recent evidence. *Housing Policy Debate* 8, 4: 833–66.

Euston, Karen. 1998. Formerly housing assistance manager, Oakland Housing Authority. Personal interview conducted by Carole C. Walker, November 9.

Feins, Judith D., Mary Joel Holin, and Antony Phipps. 1994. *Moving to Opportunity for Fair Housing Demonstration Program operations manual.* Washington, DC: U.S. Department of Housing and Urban Development.

Feins, Judith D., W. Eugene Rizor, Paul Elwood, and Linda Noel. 1997. *State and metropolitan administration of Section 8: Current models and potential resources. Final report.* April. Washington, DC: U.S. Department of Housing and Urban Development.

Finkel, Meryl, and Larry Buron. 2001. *Study on Section 8 voucher success rates. Volume I, Quantitative study of success rates in metropolitan areas.* Prepared by Abt Associates Inc. Washington, DC: U.S. Department of Housing and Urban Development.

Fischer, Paul. 1999. *Section 8 and the public housing revolution: Where will families go?* Chicago: Wood Fund of Chicago.

Freeman, Lance, and Hilary Botein. 2002. Subsidized housing and neighborhood impacts: A theoretical discussion and review of the evidence. *Journal of Planning Literature* 16, 3: 339–78.

Frieden, Bernard J. 1985. Housing allowances: An experiment that worked. In *Federal housing policy & programs*, ed. J. Paul Mitchell. New Brunswick, NJ: Center for Urban Policy Research.

Galster, George C. 2002. Trans-Atlantic perspectives on opportunity, deprivation, and the housing nexus. *Housing Studies* 17, 1: 5–10.

Galster, George C., Peter Tatian, and Robin Smith. 1999. The impact of neighbors who use Section 8 Certificates on property values. *Housing Policy Debate* 10, 4: 879–918.

Gautreaux v. Chicago Housing Authority. 1969. 304 F.Supp. 736, enforcing 296 F.Supp. 907, N.D. IL 1969.

Goering, John, and Judith D. Feins, eds. 2003. *Choosing a better life? Evaluating the Moving to Opportunity social experiment.* Washington, DC: Urban Institute Press.

Goering, John, Judith D. Feins, and Todd Richardson. 2002. A cross-site analysis of initial MTO demonstration results. *Journal of Housing Research* 13, 1: 1–30.

Goering, John, Joan Kraft, Judith D. Feins, Debra McInnis, Mary Joel Holin, and Huda Elhassan. 1999. *Moving to Opportunity for Fair Housing Demonstration Program.* Washington, DC: U.S. Department of Housing and Urban Development.

Goering, John, Helene Stebbings, and Michael Siewert. 1995. *Promoting housing choice in HUD's rental assistance programs: Report to Congress.* Washington, DC: U.S. Department of Housing and Urban Development.

Goetz, Edward G. 2002. Forced relocation vs. voluntary mobility: The effects of dispersal programs on households. *Housing Studies* 17, 1: 107–23.

———. 2003. *Clearing the Way: Deconcentrating the poor in urban America.* Washington, DC: Urban Institute Press.

Hartung, John M., and Jeffrey R. Henig. 1997. Housing vouchers and certificates as a vehicle for deconcentrating the poor: Evidence from the Washington, D.C., metropolitan area. *Urban Affairs Review* 32: 403–19.

Hollman v. Cisneros. D.MN, No. 492712. Stipulation and Amended Consent Decree, Amendment No. 3, May 13, 1998.

Housing Law Center. 1997. Latest decision on *Gautreaux v. Chicago Housing Authority. Housing Law Bulletin* 27, 10. http://www.nhlp.org/html/hlb/1097/1097gautreaux.htm.

Husock, Howard. 2000. Let's end housing vouchers. *City Journal* 10, 4: 84–91.

Iber, Robert. 1996. Chief, Multifamily Asset Division, U.S. Department of Housing and Urban Development. Personal interview conducted by David Varady, Baltimore, April 29.

Jennings, Stephanie A., and Roberto G. Quercia. 2001. Comment on Bruce J. Katz and Margery Austin Turner's "Who should run the housing voucher program? A reform proposal." *Housing Policy Debate* 12, 2: 291–98.

Johnson, Michael P., Helen F. Ladd, and Jens Ludwig. 2002. The benefits and costs of residential mobility programs for the poor. *Housing Studies* 17, 1: 125–38.

Katz, Bruce J., and Margery Austin Turner. 2001. Who should run the housing voucher program? A reform proposal. *Housing Policy Debate* 12, 2: 239–62.

Katz, Lawrence F., Jeffrey R. Kling, and Jeffrey B. Liebman. 2001. Moving to Opportunity in Boston: Early results of a randomized mobility experiment. *Quarterly Journal of Economics* 116, 2: 607–54.

Kearns, Ade. 2002. Response: From residential disadvantage to opportunity? Reflections on British and European policy and research. *Housing Studies* 17, 1: 145–50.

Kelley, Donna. 1996. Former asset manager, U.S. Department of Housing and Urban Development, Baltimore. Telephone interview conducted by David Varady, August 12.

Khadduri, Jill. 2001. Deconcentration: What do we mean? What do we want? *Cityscape* 5, 2: 69–84.

Kingsley, G. Thomas, Jennifer Johnson, and Kathy Pettit. 2000. *Housing choice for HOPE VI relocatees*, Report for the U.S. Department of Housing and Urban Development. Washington, DC: Urban Institute.

Kleit, Rachel Garshick. 2001a. Neighborhood relations in suburban scattered-site and clustered public housing. *Journal of Urban Affairs* 23, 3–4: 409–30.

———. 2001b. The role of neighborhood social networks in scattered-site public housing residents' search for jobs. *Housing Policy Debate* 12, 3: 541–73.

———. 2002. Job search networks and strategies in scattered-site public housing. *Housing Studies* 17, 1: 83–100.

Knox, Paul L. 1994. *Urbanization: An introduction to urban geography*. Englewood Cliffs, NJ: Prentice-Hall.

Kunkle, Fredrick. 2002. Housing vouchers no magic key. *Washington Post*, August 5: A1.

Lee, Chang-Moo, Dennis P. Culhane, and Susan M. Wachter. 1999. The differential impacts of federally assisted housing programs on nearby property values: A Philadelphia case study. *Housing Policy Debate* 10, 1: 75–94.

Ludwig, Jens, Greg J. Duncan, and Paul Hirschfield. 2001. Urban poverty and juvenile crime: Evidence from a randomized housing-mobility experiment. *Quarterly Journal of Economics* 116, 2: 655–80.

Ludwig, Jens, Helen F. Ladd, and Greg J. Duncan. 2001. Urban poverty and educational outcomes. *Brookings-Wharton Papers on Urban Affairs*, 147–201.

MacDonald, Heather. 1997. Comment on Sandra J. Newman and Ann B. Schnare's " '. . . And a suitable living environment': The failure of housing programs to deliver on neighborhood quality." *Housing Policy Debate* 8, 4: 755–62.

Macek, Nathan M., Asad J. Khattak, and Roberto G. Quercia. 2001. *What is the effect of commute times on employment? An analysis of the spatial patterns in the New York metropolitan area.* Washington, DC: Transportation Research Board.

Maryland–National Capitol Park and Planning Commission. n.d. Government mandated or facilitated development programs. http://www.mc-mncppc.org/research/analysis/housing/affordable/CH3.pdf.

McClure, Kirk 2001. Homebuyer and rental assistance: How do these programs affect the concentration of black households? Paper presented at the 43rd Annual Conference of the Association of Collegiate Schools of Planning, Cleveland.

Mitchell, J. Paul. 1985. Historical overview of direct federal housing assistance. In *Federal housing policy & programs*, ed. J. Paul Mitchell. New Brunswick, NJ: Center for Urban Policy Research.

Musterd, Sako. 2002. Response: Mixed housing policy: A European (Dutch) perspective. *Housing Studies* 17, 1: 139–43.

Newman, Sandra J., and Ann B. Schnare. 1997. ". . . and a suitable living environment": The failure of housing programs to deliver on neighborhood quality. *Housing Policy Debate* 8, 4: 703–42.

Olesker, Michael. 1996. Couple tapes collapse of neighborhood. *Baltimore Sun,* April 28: 1B, 6B.

Orfield, Myron. 1997. *Metropolitics: A regional agenda for community and stability.* Washington, DC: Brookings Institution Press.

Orr, Larry, Judith D. Feins, Robin Jacob, Erik Beecroft, Lisa Sanbonmatsu, Lawrence F. Katz, Jeffrey B. Liebman, and Jeffrey R. Kling. 2003. *Moving to Opportunity for Fair Housing Demonstration: Interim impacts evaluation.* Prepared by Abt Associates Inc. and National Bureau of Economic Research for U.S. Department of Housing and Urban Development, September. Washington, DC: U.S. Department of Housing and Urban Development.

Popkin, Susan J. 2002. *The Hope VI program—What about the residents?* Washington, DC: Urban Institute. http://www.urbn.org/url.cfm?ID=310593.

Popkin, Susan J., Larry F. Buron, Diane K. Levy, and Mary K. Cunningham. 2000. The Gautreaux legacy: What might mixed-income and dispersal strategies mean for the poorest public housing tenants? *Housing Policy Debate* 11, 4: 911–42.

Popkin, Susan J, and Mary K. Cunningham. 2000. *Searching for rental housing with Section 8 in the Chicago region.* Washington, DC: Urban Institute. http://www.urban.org/UploadedPDF/410314.pdf.

Popkin, Susan J., Mary K. Cunningham, Erin Godfrey, Beata Bednarz, Alicia Lewis, Janet L. Smith, Anne Knepler, and Doug Schenkleberg. 2002. *CHA relocation counseling assessment.* Report by Urban Institute for MacArthur Foundation. Washington, DC: Urban Institute.

Popkin, Susan J., Mary K. Cunningham, and William T. Woodley. 2003. *Residents at risk: A profile of Ida B. Wells and Madden Park.* Report by Urban Institute for Ford Foundation. Washington, DC: Urban Institute.

Popkin, Susan J., George Galster, Kenneth Temkin, Carla Herbig, Diane K. Levy, and Elise Richer. 2000. *Baseline assessment of public housing desegregation cases: Cross-site draft report.* Report by Urban Institute for U.S. Department of Housing and Urban Development. Washington, DC: Urban Institute.

Popkin, Susan J., Victoria E. Gwiasda, Jean M. Amendolia, Larry Buron, and Lynn Olson. 1998. *Gauging the effects of public housing redesign: Final report on the early stages of the Horner Revitalization Initiative,* Report prepared by Urban Institute for U.S. Department of Housing and Urban Development and John D. and Catherine T. MacArthur Foundation. Washington, DC: Urban Institute.

Popkin, Susan J., Victoria E. Gwiasda, Lynn M. Olson, Dennis P. Rosenbaum, and Larry Buron. 2000. *The hidden war: Crime and the tragedy of public housing in Chicago.* New Brunswick, NJ: Rutgers University Press.

Popkin, Susan J., Laura Harris, and Mary K. Cunningham. 2002. *Families in transition: A qualitative analysis of the MTO experience.* Prepared by Urban Institute for U.S. Department of Housing and Urban Development under subcontract with Abt Associates Inc. Washington, DC: U.S. Department of Housing and Urban Development.

Popkin, Susan J., Diane K. Levy, Laura E. Harris, Jennifer Comey, Mary K. Cunningham, and Larry Buron. 2002. *HOPE VI Panel Study: Baseline report.* Report prepared by Urban Institute for Annie E. Casey Foundation, John D. and Catherine T. MacArthur Foundation, Rockefeller Foundation, and U.S. Department of Housing and Urban Development. Washington, DC: Urban Institute.

Quane, James M., Bruce H. Rankin, and Pamela Joshi. 2002. Housing assistance, housing costs, and welfare reform. In *Welfare, children, & families: A three-city study.* Johns Hopkins University. Policy brief 02–4 July. http://www.jhu.edu/~welfare/20012Brief_Jun02.pdf.

Recent Research Results. 1995. Characteristics of households in public and assisted housing. U.S. Department of Housing and Urban Development, December 4, 4.

Rosenbaum, Emily, and Laura E. Harris. 2001. Residential mobility and opportunities: Early impacts of the Moving to Opportunity Demonstration program in Chicago. *Housing Policy Debate* 12, 2: 321–46.

Rosenbaum, James E. 1991. Black pioneers: Do their moves to the suburbs increase economic opportunity for mothers and children? *Housing Policy Debate* 2, 4: 179–213.

———. 1993. Closing the gap: Does racial integration improve the employment and education of low-income blacks? In *Affordable Housing and Public Policy,* ed. Lawrence B. Joseph. Chicago: University of Illinois Press.

———. 1995. Changing the geography of opportunity by expanding residential choice: Lessons from the Gautreaux program. *Housing Policy Debate* 6, 1: 231–69.

———. 1998. Gautreaux Program. In *The Encyclopedia of Housing*, ed. Willem van Vliet. Thousand Oaks, CA: Sage Publications.

Rosenbaum, James E., and Stefanie DeLuca. 2000. *Is housing mobility the key to welfare reform? Lessons from Chicago's Gautreaux program.* Washington, DC: Brookings Institution Press.

Rosenbaum, James E., Lisa Reynolds, and Stefanie DeLuca. 2002. How do places matter? The geography of opportunity, self-efficacy and a look inside the black box of residential opportunity. *Housing Studies* 17, 1: 71–82.

Rosenbaum, James E., Linda K. Stroh, and Cathy A. Flynn. 1996. Lake Parc Place: A study of mixed income housing. *Housing Policy Debate* 9, 4: 703–40.

Rubinowitz, Leonard S., and James E. Rosenbaum. 2000. *Crossing the class and color line: From public housing to white suburbia.* Chicago: University of Chicago Press.

Salama, Jerry J. 1999. The redevelopment of distressed public housing: Early results from HOPE VI projects in Atlanta, Chicago, and San Antonio. *Housing Policy Debate* 10, 1: 95–142.

Sard, Barbara. 2001. Housing vouchers should be a major component of future housing policy for the lowest income families. *Cityscape* 5, 2: 89–110.

Schrader, Carol. 1996. Multifamily information specialist, formerly asset manager, U.S. Department of Housing and Urban Development, Richmond Field Office, Richmond, VA. Telephone interview conducted by Carole C. Walker, September 5.

Schwartz, Alex, and Kian Tajbakhsh. 2001. Mixed-income housing as social policy: The case for diminished expectations. Paper presented at 43rd Annual Conference Association of Collegiate Schools of Planning, November 8, Cleveland.

Sigelman, Lee, and Jeffrey R. Henig. 2001. Crossing the great divide: Race and preferences for living in the city versus the suburbs. *Urban Affairs Review* 37: 3–18.

Smith, Robin. 2002. *Housing choice for HOPE VI relocatees.* Prepared by Urban Institute for U.S. Department of Housing and Urban Development. Washington, DC: Urban Institute.

Solomon, Arthur P., and Chester G. Fenton. 1973. *The nation's first experience with housing allowances: The Kansas City demonstration.* Cambridge, MA: Joint Center for Urban Studies of Massachusetts Institute of Technology and Harvard University.

Squires, Gregory D. 2002. Review of *Crossing the class and color lines: From public housing to white suburbia* by Leonard S. Rubinowitz and James E. Rosenbaum. *Journal of Urban Affairs* 24, 3: 369–75.

Squires, Gregory D., Samantha Friedman, and Catherine E. Saidat. 2001. Experiencing residential segregation: A contemporary study of Washington, D.C. Paper presented at International Seminar on Segregation in the City, Lincoln Institute of Land Policy, July 26–28, Cambridge, MA.

State of California. Department of Education. 2000. Educational Demographics Unit. Sacramento. http://data1.cde.ca.gov//Dataquest.

State of California. Office of the Attorney General, Criminal Justice Statistics Center. 2000. Criminal statistics, table 11. http://caag.state.ca.us/cjsc.html.

Swope, Christopher. 2002. Subsidizing blight. *Governing*, May 15, 8: 34–38.

Thompson, Richelle. 2002. Mixing neighbors, remaking communities. *Cincinnati Enquirer*, February 24. http://enquirer.com/editions/2002/02/24/loc_mixing_neighbors.html.

Turner, Margery Austin. 1998. Moving out of poverty: Expanding mobility and choice through tenant-based housing assistance. *Housing Policy Debate* 9, 2: 373–94.

Turner, Margery Austin, Susan Popkin, and Mary Cunningham. 2000. *Section 8 mobility and neighborhood health: Emerging issues and policy challenges*. Washington, DC: Urban Institute.

Turner, Margery Austin, and Kale Williams. 1998. Assisted housing mobility: Realizing the promise. Washington, DC: Urban Institute.

U.S. Bureau of the Census. 1990. U.S. Census Lookup. Tape file 3A. *http://venus.census.gov/cdrom/doc/lookup_doc.html*.

U.S. Department of Housing and Urban Development. 1999. *A house in order: Results from the first national assessment of HUD housing, April 1999*. http://www.hud.gov:80/pressrel/reacrept.html.

———. 2000. *Section 8 tenant-based housing assistance: A look back after 30 years*. Washington, DC: U.S. Department of Housing and Urban Development.

———. 2001. Housing choice vouchers fact sheet. http://www.hud.gov/offices/pih/programs/hcv/about/fact_sheet.cfm.

U.S. House of Representatives. 1970. Housing and Development Act of 1970. 91st Cong., 2nd sess. H.R. 19436.

———. 1998. Public Housing Reform Act of 1998. 105th Cong., 2nd sess. H.R. 4194.

U.S. Senate. 1937. United States Housing Act of 1937. 75th Cong., 1st sess. S. 1685.

———. 1974. Housing and Community Development Act of 1974. 93rd Cong., 2nd sess. S. 3006.

Vale, Lawrence J. 1997. Empathological places: Residents' ambivalence toward remaining in public housing. *Journal of Planning Education and Research* 16, 3:159–76.

Varady, David P., and Carole C. Walker. 1998. *Case studies of vouchered-out properties*. Prepared by Center for Urban Policy Research, Rutgers University, for U.S. Department of Housing and Urban Development. Washington, DC: U.S. Department of Housing and Urban Development.

———. 1999a. Does moving lead to enhanced feelings of safety? *Environment and Behavior* 31, 1: 3–27.

———. 1999b. Helping families move: Relocation counseling for housing voucher recipients. *Netherlands Journal of Housing and the Built Environment* 14, 1: 33–59.

———. 2000a. *Case study of Section 8 rental vouchers and rental certificates in Alameda County, California.* Prepared by Center for Urban Policy Research, Rutgers University, for U.S. Department of Housing and Urban Development. Washington, DC: U.S. Department of Housing and Urban Development.

———. 2000b. Vouchering out distressed subsidized developments: Does moving lead to improvements in housing and neighborhood conditions? *Housing Policy Debate* 11, 1: 115–62.

———. 2003a. Housing vouchers and residential mobility. *Journal of Planning Literature* 18, 1: 17–30.

———. 2003b. Using housing vouchers to move to the suburbs: The Alameda County, California, experience. *Urban Affairs Review* 39, 2: 143–80.

———. 2003c. Using housing vouchers to move to the suburbs: How do families fare? *Housing Policy Debate* 14, 3: 347–82.

Varady, David P., Carole A. Walker, and Xinhao Wang. 2001. Voucher recipient achievement of improved housing conditions in the U.S.: Do moving distance and relocation services matter? *Urban Studies* 38, 8: 1273–304.

von Hoffman, Alexander. 1998. High ambitions: The past and future of American low-income housing policy. In *New directions in urban public housing*, ed. David P. Varady, Wolfgang F.E. Preiser, and Francis P. Russell. New Brunswick, NJ: Center for Urban Policy Research.

Wasserman, Miriam. 2001. The geography of life's chances. *Regional Review* 11, 4. http://www.bos.frb.org/economic/nerr/rr2001/q4/chances.htm.

Wiest, Kurt. 1998. Deputy director, Alameda County Housing Authority, Alameda County, CA. Personal interview conducted by David Varady, December 8.

Welfeld, Irving. 1998. Gautreaux: Baby steps to opportunity. In *New directions in urban public housing*, ed. David P. Varady, Wolfgang F.E. Preiser, and Francis P. Russell. New Brunswick, NJ: Center for Urban Policy Research.

Whitehead, Christine. 2002. Response: Housing tenure and mobility. *Housing Studies* 17, 1: 63–70.

Williams, Cassaundra. 1996. Relocation counselor, Newport News, VA. Telephone interview conducted by Carole C. Walker, July 9.

Wilson, William Julius. 1987. *The truly disadvantaged: The inner city, the underclass, and public policy.* Chicago: University of Chicago Press.

Yin, Robert. 1994. *Case study research: Design and methods.* Thousand Oaks, CA: Sage Publications.

Yinger, John. 1998. Housing discrimination is worth worrying about. *Housing Policy Debate* 9, 4: 893–927.

Index

A

Abt Associates, 12
Aid to Families with Dependent
  Children (AFDC), 44
Alameda County, California
  housing and neighborhood condi-
    tions, *116, 117*
  housing counseling, 13
  housing search, *112–113*
  housing search satisfaction, *114, 115*
  housing voucher program, 4
  Section 8 families, *107, 108*
  Section 8 program, 2, 3
  study site, *106,* 111–121, 160–162
  suburbs, vouchers and move to, 105–
    110, 163–164
    adjustment issues, 139
    counseling, 3
    distance moved, 135
    explanations for moves, 131–134
    housing, searching for, 121–131
    housing and neighborhood
      conditions, 139–150
    housing and neighborhood
      satisfaction, 150–152
    migration patterns, 134–138
    research strategy, 110–111
Albany, California, 120
Amsterdam, the Netherlands, 23
ARCO, 47
Ashland, California, 118, 120, 136
Atkinson, Rowland, 23
automobile access, 128–129, 157–158n
    22. *See also* reverse commut-
    ing

Note: Italicized page numbers refer to
tables and figures.

B

Baltimore, Maryland
  clustering, 20
  discrimination, 80–81
  Eutaw Gardens, *35–42,* 44–54, 65–
    67, 97, 160
  house values, 72
  housing search, 73, 80
  Moving to Opportunity demonstra-
    tion, 10, 11–12
Baltimore County, Maryland, 20, 81
BART. *See* Bay Area Rapid Transit
Basgal, Ophelia, 13
Bay Area Rapid Transit (BART), 118,
    120
Berkeley, California, 2
  neighborhoods, *119*
  Section 8 program, 3
  study site, 111–121
  suburbs, vouchers and move to, 105–
    110, 163
    adjustment issues, 139
    counseling, 3
    explanations for moves, 131–134
    housing, searching for, 121–131
    housing and neighborhood
      conditions, 139–150
    housing and neighborhood
      satisfaction, 150–152
    migration patterns, 134–138
    research strategy, 110–111
Berkeley Housing Authority (BHA),
    120
BHA. *See* Berkeley Housing Authority
Boston, Massachusetts, 10, 11, 16, 73
Bronx (New York City), 22
Brophy, Paul, 22
Buron, Larry, 18